MW00668750

MUSSOLINI'S SOLDIERS

REX TRYE
MUSSOLINI'S SOLDIERS

Motorbooks International
Publishers & Wholesalers ®

In memory of Carlo Rocchio, friend and fellow
collector of Italian militaria, and his wife Suzie,
who both died accidentally, tragically in 1987

This edition first published in 1995 by Motorbooks International,
Publishers & Wholesalers, PO Box 2, 729 Prospect Avenue,
Osceola, WI 54020, USA.

© Rex Trye, 1995

Previously published by Airlife Publishing Ltd., Shrewsbury, England, 1995

All rights reserved. With the exception of quoting brief passages
for the purposes of review no part of this publication may be
reproduced without prior written permission from the publisher.

Motorbooks International is a certified trademark,
registered with the United States Patent Office.

The information in this book is true and complete to the best of
our knowledge. All recommendations are made without any
guarantee on the part of the author or publisher, who also disclaim
any liability incurred in connection with the use of this data or
specific details.

We recognize that some words, model names and designations,
for example, mentioned herein are the property of the trademark
holder. We use them for identification purposes only. This is not
an official publication.

Motorbooks International books are also available at discounts in
bulk quantity for industrial or sales-promotional use. For details
write to Special Sales Manager at the publisher's address.

Library of Congress Cataloging-in-Publication Data is available

ISBN 0-7603-0022-4

Printed and bound in Singapore.

Table of Contents

Introduction   7

Foreword   8

Acknowledgements   9

Chapter One – The Citizen Soldier   11
The rise of Mussolini; The Citizen Soldier; Conscripts; Semi-combat elements; Conscripts' training;
Warrant officer and NCO training; Officers and their training; System of promotion for officers;
Rations; Burials and graves.

Chapter Two – Army Organisation   39
Infantry divisions; Mobile (cavalry) divisions; Armoured divisions; Motorised divisions; Paratroops;
Field artillery; Engineers; Chemical troops; Frontier guard; The Militias; Support services.

Chapter Three – Combat Uniforms   59
Continental uniforms; Tropical uniforms; Specialised paratroop garments; Protective clothing.

Chapter Four – Headwear   97
Steel helmets; Crash helmets; Continental peak caps; Continental side caps; Tropical peaked caps;
Tropical side caps; Pith helmets; Alpine caps; Fez.

Chapter Five – Small-Arms and Field Equipment   109
Artillery service; Model 35, 20/65 AA gun (Breda); Model 37, 47/32 anti-tank gun; 65/17 infantry gun;
Mortars; Hand grenades; Revolvers and pistols; Machine-guns; Rifles; Bayonets and combat daggers;
Holsters and bandoliers; Knapsacks, rucksacks and haversacks; Gasmasks; Water bottles and mess tins;
Shelter quarters; Miscellaneous; Officer accoutrements.

Chapter Six – Documents and Insignia   135
Evaluation book; Individual record book; MVSN identification booklet; Warrant officer and officer pay
book; Military pay; Military postal service; Ranks; Collar patches and devices; Gallantry medals; Order of
precedence for wearing medals; Identity discs; Arm shields; Fascist Militia Zone shields; Militia shields.

Chapter Seven – Armistice 1943, The beginning of the end   153

Glossary   159

Bibliography   163

Index   165

Introduction

For a number of years I have been a collector of Italian Fascist era militaria. As I grew more involved in the subject I became acutely aware of the sad fact that many of the pieces in my collection would not have survived or would have languished unrecognised had I not obtained them from the servicemen who originally brought them back as souvenirs from World War II. In the next decade there is going to be even less available for collectors, so I think it is important that all information that still survives is recorded for the sake of future generations before it is gone forever.

This book will, I hope, add to the understanding and study of the Italian army during the period the Fascist Party was in power. Both the Royal Army and the Fascist Militias are examined – their organisation, arms, uniforms and equipment. Items illustrated in this book are genuine pieces taken from my collection and the collections of friends.

It would take many volumes to deal with every aspect of this subject fully. I have, therefore, been forced to touch only lightly on some areas. I have, however, endeavoured to cover all the salient points sufficiently so that an intelligible overall picture is painted for the reader.

Along the way I hope to have redressed some of the misconceptions about the fighting capabilities of the Italian armed forces – the fact that many of them have survived into the post-war generations shows the effectiveness of Allied propaganda targeted against the Italians during World War II.

By examining the system under which the Italians operated, the logistic problems encountered and the succession of conflicts in which Italy was involved before and during World War II, a clearer understanding can be gleaned. Written on an Italian monument near El Alamein in North Africa are the words 'Luck was missing, not valour'; while larger events often overtook the Italian soldier, his individual bravery was not lacking.

Benito Mussolini boasted to have 'eight million bayonets', though Maresciallo Rodolfo Graziani best summed up Italy's true military situation when he said, 'You cannot break armour with fingernails alone . . .'

Foreword

WHEN REX TRYE kindly asked me to put my pen to work on the introduction for this book, I felt honoured. Mr Trye had, during the gruelling and exhaustive research for his book, interviewed my late father, Antonio D'Angelo, who recalled his military experiences, under Mussolini's rule, with great relish. He himself was impressed that a non-Italian would even embark on such a venture – to write about the Italian soldier, his shortcomings, his triumphs, his grief and his courage in the face of overwhelming odds in the last war.

I somehow felt inadequate to put my remarks in this book in view of the many people more qualified than I. But I have researched and collected, written and debated the Italian contribution for the last thirty years, and so when Rex embarked on this work, I was thrilled as well as reserved for I knew he had his work cut out for him. Sadly, there are few books on the Italian soldiers' experience outside of Italy itself, which is obsessed with its military history, from the Roman Empire to Mussolini's attempt to rebuild the Second Roman Empire. Books on the German experience and the equipment from tanks to swords are in abundance, but pitifully few have surfaced on Italy. It is my sincere belief, as I pored over this arduous work, that this will be the start of a long and continued thrust to bring the Italian militaria and Italy's wartime experiences, both positive and negative, into a more clear and concise focus.

Rex has expertly woven in with the memories and remarks of the Italian soldier, serious research and identification of weaponry and the vast number of uniforms and accoutrements the Italians put in the field.

This interest in Italian military history and militaria has come a long way in the past decade and it continues to grow at a rapid pace. Rex Trye has made that interest more in-depth, and also by putting forth the human experience of those brave soldiers who have often been maligned and misunderstood, shatters the negative portrayal of the Italian fighting man. While the Italian soldier was never the warlike and military fighting machine of his allies, Germany and Japan, he was above all a man dedicated to life, love and family, his country and his god. And the vast number of casualties that Italy suffered in both World Wars proved that the Italian soldier was not afraid to die with 'Viva Italia' and 'Viva il Duce' on his lips. The Italian soldier went above and beyond the call of duty, of human endurance, given the terrain, equipment, training and leadership (or lack thereof) that he was exposed to. In the motto of the Royal Carabinieri, it was to 'Obey silently and to die silently'. Luck, not valour, was missing from the battlefield.

Every historian, military collector and enthusiast will certainly broaden his understanding and knowledge once he has absorbed the contents of this study. We, collectively, and I, personally, owe Rex Trye deep gratitude for this valuable reference, sure to be an often quoted work into this fascinating period of history.

Rudy A. D'Angelo
Farmington, Connecticut
USA

Acknowledgements

T HE PERIOD in which Mussolini held the reins of power in Italy has been a subject of deep fascination to me for over a decade through my collection of Italian military memorabilia. I sincerely hope to have portrayed this interest through the text and photographs enclosed herein.

Dal McGuirk actively assisted me in gathering photos to use as illustrations and generously gave me photos from his own collection covering the North African campaign. A great many people have helped me in so many ways during the writing of this book, all of whose input has contributed towards a greater understanding on my part of the subject.

So to all of you who have helped me along the way I say most humbly *grazie!*

In alphabetical order: Sergio Andreanelli; the late Claudio Andreanelli; Rudy D'Angelo; the late Antonio D'Angelo; Piero Assenza; Aldo Bacoccoli; Peter Battistan; Enrico Buffoni; Wayne Butler; Carlo Breschi; Luigi Bonechi; Paolo Bronzi; Antonio Cioci; Peter Coleman; Giovanni Costa; Denis Culverwell; John Daymond; N. V. Dooling; Libro Di Zinno; Giuseppe Fassio; Franco Fassio; Franco Festa; Giuseppe Festa; Giuseppe Fichera; Cosmo Fragnito; Jack Hobbs; Dieter Hellriegel; Bob Holt; Clem Kelly; Thanas Laske; Mario Lanteri; Tullio Lisignoli; Antoine Lebel; Giovanino Laterza; Dick and Patsy LaFayette; Jack McCook; Dal and Christine McGuirk; Otto Meyer; Aldo Nava; Dave Oldham; Geoff Oldham; Alberto Priero; Marco Penessi; the late Carlo and Suzie Rocchio; Achille Rastelli; Ian Rasmusen; Ray Richards; Giorgio Sabatini; Aldo Sbrissa; Susan Sbrenna; Frank and Jessie Trye; Hugh Page Taylor; Phil Whernham.

Chapter One
The Citizen Soldier

Benito Mussolini, Dictator of Fascist Italy and its colonial empire.
(Author's collection)

The Rise of Mussolini

Benito Amilcare Andrea Mussolini was born on 29 July 1883 in a humble hamlet near the commune of Predappio in the rugged region of Romagna in north-eastern Italy, the eldest child of the local schoolmistress Rosa and her husband Alessandro Mussolini, a blacksmith. Alessandro was a politically active and ardent socialist and anti-cleric whose views were so strong that he named his eldest son after three left-wing revolutionaries of the time.

Young Mussolini grew up embracing his father's political beliefs and in early adulthood lived a bohemian life as a socialist agitator, being imprisoned numerous times for his activities. He was of less than medium height, stocky with thinning black hair (which he was later to shave off completely), dark brown piercing eyes, a long face with a jutting chin which he thrust upwards to give himself the appearance of being taller than he was. Though a qualified school teacher, he drifted through various job as a labourer and latterly as a journalist, becoming editor of the socialist newspaper *Avanti*. He was expelled from the Socialist Party in 1914 when he publicly supported Italy's involvement in World War I, contrary to the party's stated policy that Italy should remain neutral in the conflict.

In 1915, with Italy's entry into World War I on the side of the Allies, Mussolini was conscripted into the 11 Bersaglieri Regiment. In 1902 he had left Italy to live in Switzerland. During the period that followed he was found guilty in his absence of desertion from the army by an Italian court as he had not returned to do his eighteen months' military service. With a general amnesty declared for deserters in late 1904 he returned to Italy and in 1905 served his time as a model soldier in the 10 Bersaglieri Regiment at Verona.

Life as a front-line soldier in the desolate, rocky and wet trenches of the Alpine front facing the Austrians was hard, though Mussolini served with little complaint, attaining the rank of corporal. His military service ended abruptly when an Italian mortar shell exploded prematurely during a test firing. Mussolini was badly wounded with numerous shrapnel splinters, and was invalided out of the army in 1917.

Italy emerged from World War I with 600,000 dead, and one-and-a-half million wounded, a huge war debt and a shattered economy with rampant inflation. It was against this background that on 23 March 1919 the embryo Fascist movement with its anti-socialist aims had its humble beginnings in a hall in Milan's Piazza San Sepolcro. The meeting was attended by a handful of ex-soldiers, disillusioned socialists, idealists, political opportunists and adventurers.

The symbol of this fledgling organisation was the *Fascio*, originally found in an Etruscan tomb in 7 BC by the Romans, who adapted it for their own use. It consisted of a bundle of elm rods tied together with red cord to an axe, symbolising the military and judicial powers of the empire. They were carried by *littori* (Roman officers who accompanied high-ranking judges) on the left shoulder. Mussolini modified these meanings – the bundle of rods, he said, represented the unity of the people and the axe signified strength.

Support for this radical group with strong right-wing tendencies (a total about-turn politically from Mussolini's earlier views) slowly grew throughout Italy. Aided through the pages of *Popolo d'Italia* (the opposition newspaper he managed to start in Milan after his expulsion from the Socialist Party) Mussolini began to mobilise a personal following backed by a private army of ex-soldiers and thugs known as *squadristi*, men who had no hesitation in employing strong-arm tactics against their socialist opposition – or anyone else who was seen to oppose them. Among the favourite methods used by the *squadristi* was forcing the victim to swallow a bottle of castor oil (known as Fascist medicine) and the liberal use of a short, stout wooden bludgeon known as a *manganello*.

Support for the Fascist Party grew to such an extent that in the 1921 elections thirty-four seats in the parliamentary Chamber of Deputies were won by Fascist candidates, one of whom was Benito Mussolini.

A real opportunity for Mussolini to seize power from the Liberal Party under Prime Minister Luigi Facta came in 1922 when the socialists called a general strike. Mussolini used this as a pretext to act and

Blackshirt squadristi in Bologna wear a mixture of civilian and military clothing in this photograph taken in the 1920s. Several are wearing the blackshirt of the Arditi. Also in evidence is the wooden manganello cudgel used by the blackshirts. (Author's collection)

Vittorio Emanuele III, King of Italy and Albania, Emperor of Ethiopia. (Author's collection)

declared that unless the government broke the strike the Fascists would; he also demanded they be given control of the government or he and his Blackshirts (*squadristi*) would march on Rome and seize power. The government chose to ignore this warning.

Columns of Blackshirts approximately 40,000 strong moved from the north and south of Italy towards Rome. Many were so poorly equipped they could easily have been routed by the police and army if the order had been given. Instead the huge bluff worked and Mussolini was invited to form a government by King Vittorio Emanuele III.

Vittorio Emanuele was born on 11 November 1869 in Naples, the son of Umberto I di Savoia and his wife Margherita di Savoia-Genova. Vittorio Emanuele inherited the crown in 1900 after his father was shot and killed by an Italian peasant's son in the northern town of Monza.

The king was physically a small man, barely five feet tall (Mussolini, although short himself, was taller than the king and liked to be photographed next to him.) Nicknamed 'little sword', he was timid, very distrustful though shrewd, and thrifty to the point of meanness. His main private interests in life were the royal house of Savoy, his wife Queen Elena (daughter of King Nikita of Montenegro), his extensive and very valuable coin collection and a passion for hunting.

Mussolini became the sixth Prime Minister in three years. The new government he formed contained members from all the main political groups, with only a few Fascists included. In the 1924 election the Fascist Party polled 65 per cent of the votes. By 1925 the opposition parties were rendered virtually powerless due to the often violent and repressive methods used against them by Fascists. On 3 January 1925 Mussolini had announced in Parliament his intention to take sole

Credere, Obbedire, Combattere – Believe, Obey, Fight. Mussolini's battle cry was publicly displayed throughout Italy. (Author's collection)

responsibility for the righting of Italy's woes through his personal leadership – in essence a dictatorship. In 1926 all political parties except the Fascists were formally abolished by Mussolini, who thus paved the way for a truly Fascist regime. Heralded by many as the beginning of the second Roman Empire, it dominated almost every aspect of Italian life for the next seventeen years.

A column of L3 tankettes pass the Triumphal Arch in Rome during a parade of 50,000 Italian troops before Adolf Hitler during his May 1938 visit to Italy. Fascism was heralded by many as the beginning of the second Roman Empire. (Author's collection)

Although under the Italian constitution the king was supreme commander of all military forces, in peace he entrusted those powers to a Minister of War, under the Prime Minister. In wartime a supreme commander was appointed with the advice of Cabinet. But under the Fascist regime, Mussolini – as Prime Minister and also Minister of War, Marine and Air – rivalled the monarch for control of the military. Under a thin veneer of serving a constitutional monarchy, Mussolini was to all intents and purposes *Duce* (leader) of Fascist Italy.

The Citizen Soldier

In the Fascist state the functions of the citizen and soldier were regarded as inseparable. Military training was considered an integral part of national education. It began as soon as male citizens were capable of learning and continued as long as they were able to carry arms.

The first phase was pre-service instruction, with the object of preparing a citizen morally, physically and militarily for joining the armed forces.

In 1919 the first formations of the Italian Youth Brigades appeared. Called the Student Vanguard, they were in 1921 renamed Fascist Youth Vanguards or AGF. From October 1922 these first groups of youths aged eight to fourteen were organised and given the name *Balilla*. This was the nickname of a streetboy from Genova in northern Italy who in the mid-eighteenth century as an act of defiance hurled stones at occupying Austrian soldiers. This daring exploit was cited as an example of patriotism.

In 1926, the official name *Opera Nazionale Balilla* (ONB) was constituted. The purpose of the organisation was to instil into youngsters the virtues of physical fitness, discipline, political education and semi-military training based on drills, gymnastics, parades and all form of sport.

In 1929, the ONB came under the jurisdiction of the Minister of Education and in the same year young girls were also encouraged to join. By 1935 almost all young children between the walking age of around eighteen months up to eight years were organised into the Children-of-the-She-Wolf sections.

Balilla members undergo drill at a Fascist Youth camp in Pietragallo, Italy. August 1942. (Rudy D'Angelo)

The following breakdown shows how the youth organisations operated:

BOYS: From birth to age 8 – Children-of-the-She-Wolf
From 8 to 11 – Balilla
From 11 to 14 – Balilla Musketeers
From 14 to 16 – Vanguards
From 16 to 18 – Vanguard Musketeers

GIRLS: From birth to age 8 – Children-of-the-She-Wolf
From 8 to 14 – Little Italians Feminine Gender
From 14 to 18 – Young Italians Feminine Gender

In October 1930 all youths aged eighteen to twenty-one were organised into Groups of Young Combatants (the FGC). These were placed directly under the control of the Secretary of the Fascist Party, and when its members turned twenty-one they became party members.

In 1937 the Balilla and FGC were amalgamated and renamed the Fascist Youth of the Lictors, or GIL. The group became more military as it prepared for eventual volunteers into the Fascist Militia. The ONB, under the merger, continued its pre-military training work. By 1940 the Fascist Youth was more than five million strong.

It should be noted that during the late 1920s, the ONB's growing influence over young boys was strongly resisted by the Vatican. This came about after a 1928 statute forbade the organisation of new youth groups and dissolved the Catholic Boy Scouts. While this was harshly criticised, in reality the law applied only to towns with less than 20,000 inhabitants. At the same time the nation's youth was also organised into groups called Italian Catholic Action to maintain religious and moral discipline.

With Italy's entry into World War II in 1940, the Fascist Youth managed to recruit an additional 25,000 young men aged sixteen to eighteen to train, equip and place them in military formations for combat. These Youth Battalions took the name of the provinces in which they were raised.

In the Italian colony of Libya a comparable Fascist organisation for Arab youngsters, known as Arab Youth of the Fascist Rod (GAL), was instituted in 1935. The GAL was organised into eight battalions. Four, known as *Aftal*, were for boys up to the age of twelve (like the Balilla). The others were known as *Sciubban*, for youths aged twelve to eighteen, similar to

Vanguard. Members' training was the same as the GIL in Italy and included weapons handling, although the Libyan groups were never used in a combat role.

In the East African colonies of Eritrea and Ethiopia a Fascist Youth organisation modelled on the GAL existed for native youngsters; originally called Eritrean Youth of the Fascist Rod and Ethiopian Youth of the Fascist Rod, they were after 1938 renamed the Indigenous Youth of the Fascist Rod.

In 1937 a GIL for East African and Mediterranean territories was formed. Organised along the same lines as the Italian metropolitan GIL, it was for the Italian youths resident in those territories only and was separate from the organisation for native youths.

The Albanian Fascist Youth for ethnic Albanians was formed in 1939 after the country's military occupation by Italy. It was similar to the GIL in Italy, with a Balilla and a Vanguard for boys and a separate detachment for girls. They were collectively called the New Front.

Thanas Laske, a former member of the Albanian Fascist Youth, recalls:

When the Italians occupied Albania there was resentment and some Albanians fought on three occasions, especially in the Durres Mountains. But eventually they became resigned to the occupation and things settled down.

The Italians were very friendly and not brutal to our people – we were a poor country and wanted to survive. The Italians quickly began to pacify the population, and brought in food, clothing, taught us to speak, read and write Italian, and to sing their songs. The Italian soldiers were crazy about our women. They were lovers, not fighters!

We prospered under them. They had the best propaganda machine ever. They built roads, schools, a stadium and new buildings everywhere. They were incredible and very hard workers.

Mussolini and the King of Italy were rulers and self-styled protectors of Albania. There was a motto which we had to say all the time '*Rofte – Duce – Ja*', which means 'God Bless the Duce'. On the surface we followed the Italians, but in our hearts we were still Albanian.

I belonged to both the Balilla and the GIL. I had to go to training every day and had three hours of Italian lessons daily as well. All children in the youth formations did Youth Labour Service from the age of ten and above.

My uniform was a black shirt with a red kerchief. I can recall trucks and trucks of equipment, uniforms, blankets. Everything was provided – we had to pay for nothing. The GIL officers gave many gifts to the people.

There was a large Italian military presence in Albania

during the years of occupation. The Italians were fighting the Greeks all the time, with us in between. The Italians were afraid of the Greek soldiers, however, and when the Italians fled Greece, the Greeks came into Albania and were cruel. We were left with nothing after the war and we had to pawn everything just to eat. I remember our girls would grow long braids and sell their hair. The Italians were pretty much out of Albania by 1944.

In 1930, Italian Youths Abroad for young Italians living in the USA, England and France was formed. Affiliated to the Italian GIL by the National Institution of the Sons of the Fascist Rod, they had the same organisational structure and uniforms as the GIL in Italy.

Although membership of the juvenile Fascist organisations was not strictly compulsory, many found it convenient to belong and few students missed the chance. Apart from some political involvement there was the opportunity for every youngster to participate in many sports free of charge, even the expensive ones such as horse riding, gliding, sailing or skiing. To belong cost a nominal one lira a year (membership was free to the poorer children, however). Uniforms were provided for needy youngsters, although the majority were required to buy their own from military outfitters.

The muster for youth training was mainly on Saturday afternoons, although sometimes sessions were held on Sunday mornings. Saturday afternoon was known as 'Fascist Saturday' and was considered a festive day. Sometimes a military-style meal was provided.

Every Italian province had a Federal Command which each year organised camps in which members of the Balilla, Vanguard and Young Fascists participated. There was also a large annual 'leader's camp' in Rome, to which the provinces sent their most deserving candidates. This was organised along military lines and lasted for a month.

Theoretical military instruction in schools completed the practical training given by the pre-military organisations. This aimed to make good citizen soldiers of young men through the development of military spirit, patriotism and character. School military instruction included thirty one-hour lessons annually for five scholastic years, spread from the last year of grammar school to the second year of college.

Military training in the schools was divided into three grades:

(1) First grade training covered the last year of grammar school (thirteen to fourteen-year-olds). It provided an elementary military knowledge (organisation of the Italian army, interpretation of topographical maps). Those boys not continuing their academic studies would be enlisted as NCOs or specialists such as mechanics, electricians, radio and telegraph operators, chauffeurs or motorcyclists. Use was made of movie films, photography, drawings, diagrams, etc, for instruction.

(2) Second grade training covered the last two years of high school (seventeen to eighteen-year-olds). This course taught military knowledge (organisation of the armed forces of different nations, elementary knowledge of weapons) to students who could become complementary (reserve) officers without attending university. Its purpose was to complete the first grade course, to show the connection between the military and the social and economic life of the nation, to give the youths a warlike spirit, and to teach a sense of discipline, comradeship and sacrifice.

(3) Third grade covered the first two years of college (nineteen to twenty-year-olds). This course presented material on the military preparation of a modern nation and the theory of modern warfare, with discussion of missions by the various armed forces, separately and jointly. The majority of officers for the armed forces were graduates of this course.

The pre-military training in schools and in special organisations such as the Vanguard and Fascist Youth emphasised the individual training of the soldier. Special instruction in marksmanship was offered through enrolment in the Italian Target Practice Union, which came under the control of the Chief Inspector of Pre- and Post-Military Training.

A personal evaluation booklet was instituted in 1937. This was issued to every new recruit during the Fascist call-up, which was on 28 October of each year (the anniversary of the Fascist March on Rome). It was required to be kept from the eleventh to the thirty-second year. In addition to details of the physical condition of the holder, other information such as an evaluation of the intellectual, sporting, social, political and military activities was also recorded.

Conscripts

All Italian male citizens were legally liable for military service from the age of eighteen to fifty-five. Normally, youths were called up for pre-military service during the twelve months in which they completed their eighteenth year. During World War II, however, they were conscripted at eighteen and did not undertake the normal pre-military training.

In peacetime males normally had their medical examination and were registered for conscript service in the year in which they had their twentieth birthday. The full period of service was eighteen months.

During World War II civil authorities were required to furnish the military district command (which was based on the commune area) with a list of all males who would reach eighteen years in the calendar year just beginning. In the late spring, conscripts were called for medical examination, leaving behind their identity cards and statement of pre-military service. Examinations were made in the various communes by 'mobile commissions' sent out from the district offices. The commander of each military district was responsible for the registration and drafting of conscripts and their assignment to units. He likewise maintained a list of all men furloughed to the reserve (assigned to the district company until called to active service).

All males in Italy and its colonies and those males of Italian nationality residing abroad were divided into classes in accordance with the year of their birth. For example, the class normally entering pre-military (Young Fascist) service in 1941 and military service in 1943 were known as class of 1922.

Soldiers of reserve class 1901 are called up to the colours. Milano, March 1939. (Author's collection)

A march through the streets of Rome by Blackshirts just returned from East Africa. August 1936. (Author's collection)

Within the year in which they completed their eighteenth year, all youths were called into service under the following categories:

(a) Young men for service with the Young Fascists, leading to service in the active army.
(b) Those not physically qualified for service with the Young Fascists, but who passed into limited service (coastal defences, fixed anti-aircraft defences, finance guards, etc).
(c) Those temporarily unfit who were deferred to a subsequent draft.
(d) Those permanently physically unfit, who passed into the untrained reserve. These men were practically exempt from military service, though theoretically subject to call-up in time of war and to periodic physical examination.

Exemption from active service was also given for reasons other than physical disability. These were: penal offenses, deprivation of political rights, previous enrolment in the various militias, or mental deficiency. Length of service was sometimes reduced for reasons of family need. Thus, for example, reduction could be granted to 'the only brother of an orphan sister', 'only child of a widow over sixty-four', 'first-born of a family of ten sons', etc. Students could have their service deferred until they had completed their education, but not later than the end of their twenty-sixth year. Italians born or resident in foreign countries were liable for military service but, in practice, the majority were exempted during their period of residence abroad or, under certain circumstances, would serve for only six months.

In 1942, the War Department exempted persons having dual nationality from military service if, in addition to Italian nationality, they possessed the nationality of a state at war with Italy. Italian citizens of the Aegean Islands or Libya, and the subjects of Italian East Africa, were not required to perform military service. Foreigners who had become naturalised Italian citizens were exempt from service only if over thirty-two.

Volunteers, Italian nationals and those who had the right to become such by performing military service were able to enlist if they were: seventeen and under twenty-seven years old; bachelors or widowers without children; physically fit to perform service in the corps for which they volunteered as well as military service in general; of good character and moral, i.e. not guilty of certain specified crimes; able to show parental consent; and able to read and write.

In time of war, voluntary enlistments for the duration were accepted. The Fascist Militia, Carabi-

nieri, Finance Guard and the special non-combatant organisations included in the armed forces were supported by voluntary enlistment.

Antonio D'Angelo of the 2 Divisione 28 Ottobre, 131 Legione, recalls when he volunteered for service in the Ethiopian campaign in 1935:

My mother was upset because she was a widow with four children, but she understood how I personally felt about Fascism. She was upset only from a mother's emotional viewpoint and not because she was anti-government or anti-war. The Italian public understood the war, the newsreels, photographs and propaganda for the war; its reasons; the waging of the war. It was well understood by the public both in Italy and abroad, so that a number of Italians overseas returned home to fight with us and were organised into a unit themselves – 221 Legione Fasci all' Estero.

2 battalion, Giovani Fascisti regiment on parade at the village of Gioda, Libya. 1942. (Museum Rgt. Vol. GGFF, Ponti sul Mincio, Italy)

The first large detachment of Italians to leave Spain, consisting of some 10,000 men, disembark in Naples, 1939. (Author's collection)

The Ethiopian campaign was an extremely popular patriotic war. Morale was high among the soldiers. Most felt it was a chance for Italy to have a 'place in the sun' – somewhere where the land was excellent for farming and there was plenty of room; a place where Italians could settle instead of having to emigrate to other countries.

D'Angelo remembers the reception that awaited him when he came back to Italy in 1939 after service in East Africa:

We got an excellent national welcome, with many parades. There was great military spirit among townspeople – many hugs and kisses, and the handing out of flowers. Everyone offered food and wine to returning soldiers. We were treated as heroes.

Antonio Cioci, of the Reggimento Giovani Fascisti, recounts:

Our regiment was the only one in the Royal Army composed entirely of volunteers. We were enlisted between 10 June 1940 (declaration of war) and 30 June 1940 (1st and 2nd Battalions). The volunteers of the 3rd Battalion were enlisted in January of 1942 to replace combat losses of the earlier battalions. They came from all over Italy, and were of many different social standings – from the nobleman to the countryman, and the student to the worker.

In the regiment there were a number of brothers: Regonini, Giachi, Cocchi, Niccolini. The Cocchi and Niccolini brothers played a heroic part in the battle of Bir el Gobi in Libya from 3-7 December 1941. Both Tenente Antonio Cocchi and Mario Niccolini were wounded, while their brothers Ippolito Niccolini and Giorgio Cocchi fell on the field of battle, earning the Gold Medal and Silver Medal for Military Valour respectively.

We, the Young Fascists, were the sons of Fascism. We thought a lot of Mussolini because of all the civil works and reforms that were undertaken during his government and his love of the Italian people.

After the battle of Bir el Gobi, the Giovani Fascisti Regiment was elevated to full divisional strength. It fought in the North African campaign from 1941 until 13 May 1943. It is interesting to note that Mussolini had initially wanted it to be sent to Russia, but the generals opposed him and it was posted instead to North Africa.

Sotto Tenente Giuseppe Fassio, of Motomitraglieri Battaglione, 9 Bersaglieri Reggimento, recounts:

In 1937 I was told that my platoon was chosen out of the battalion to be sent abroad. Our battalion was equipped with motorcycles [most likely Moto Guzzis] with a light machine-gun in front.

In Naples, before my departure, I was required to purchase a complete set of tropical khaki uniform and underwear. I assumed we were being sent to East Africa.

We departed Naples on 7 January 1937. When on board ship we were told the destination was Spain, where we were to fight as 'volunteers' against the communists. All rank insignia we removed from our uniforms, in case the ship was sunk, so our origin wouldn't be obvious. When we landed in Spain we put them on again.

I disembarked in Cadiz and, as part of the Bersaglieri Motomitraglieri, was attached to the Littorio Division under the command of Generale Bergonzoli. I was automatically promoted to the rank of *tenente* in command of a *plotone*, which I commanded at the battle of Malaga. Our allies, the anti-communist Spanish forces led by General Francisco Franco, known as the Falangists, fought well but the communists were badly organised.

During the battle of Guadalajara the battalion was practically destroyed and so I was transferred to the 2 Compagnia, 1 Battaglione, 1 Reggimento, Frecce Azzurre Divisione. There was good co-operation between us Italians and the Spaniards at all levels. Morale was good. However, the arms we received were from aging stocks in Italy and we were unhappy with them.

At Sierra Grana [Cerro del Toro] I was ordered to reconnoitre down a valley to check the presence of the enemy. But someone forgot to tell our soldiers about my mission and before long I was being shot at by our soldiers from a nearby mountain ridge. Then the enemy started firing at me from and opposite ridge!

I had to lie flat to avoid being shot. Eventually our men were told of my whereabouts, but I couldn't move until dark because the enemy also knew of my presence. I think I accomplished my mission anyhow, because the enemy would not have fired if his own soldiers were in the valley.

I was wounded at Sierra Grana on 21 April during an attack while I was taking cover and a bullet passed through the soft parts of my back. I received a Bronze Valour Medal for my part.

During the siege of Bilboa on 13 June 1937, at a place called Sierra Altezuela, I was again wounded. It was during a morning attack and I was hit in the right leg by a dumdum bullet. Fortunately my batman had a rope with him, so he tied my leg and left me in the shelter of a ditch.

In the meantime, Fascist aeroplanes were bombing the communist positions and a splinter hit me in the left arm as I lay there. It was late afternoon before I was taken back for treatment. I was sent to a hospital in Seville and then in July I was returned to Italy on the hospital ship *Gradisca*.

After service in the army, voluntary enlistment for two successive five-year terms in the Fascist Militia was encouraged. In theory, the ten years' service was compulsory until the age of thirty-two, but because of the lack of trained instructors in Militia ranks, the law was, for the most part, a dead letter and training of reservists was mainly carried out by periodical recall to the colours.

Antonio D'Angelo recounts his post-military service with the Fascist Militia up to 1943:

After my return from Ethiopia in June 1939 I was recalled by the Royal Army regiment with which I had undertaken my original military service, the 151 Reggimento Fanteria, Divisione Sassari, which was being trained to be sent to Greece. I elected to remain in the Blackshirts, and in August 1939 I went back to the Divisione 28 Ottobre Libica, as it was now being called, which was being mobilised for service in North Africa. When Italy declared war on Britain, my unit was in Libya and we were sent to fight the British soldiers. I was wounded at Sollum in Egypt and later at Sidi-Barrani and sent back to Italy to recover from my wounds.

I remained as a reservist with my CCNN unit in my home town until I was recalled to service in November 1941, the week after I was married. I was transferred to the Milizia Confinaria in December 1941/January 1942 and was stationed at Pisticci [southern Italy], a jail at which both criminal and political prisoners were held, until September 1943. The town was bombed by American and British forces and almost totally destroyed.

There was also provision for three-, two-, and one-year enlistments in the armed forces. The three-year enlistments were: soldiers of certain units re-enlisting after completion of service; volunteers or transfers to the Carabinieri; corporals in the remount service; musicians on active service, but not NCOs.

The two-year enlistments were: volunteers in arms and corps exclusive of Carabinieri; volunteers in auxiliary Carabinieri (excluding transfers from other arms); corporals and other ranks re-enlisting after completion of service.

The one-year enlistments were: soldiers in all arms and services could be retained in service for one or more years if necessary; specialists who received a bonus of two or more lire a day; certain headquarters soldiers could re-enlist for a period of one year with or without a bonus or three years with a bonus.

Soldiers whose period of service was complete continued in the reserve until their fifty-fifth year.

Semi-Combat Elements

The Royal Carabinieri or CCRR, commonly called the 'first arm of the army', was a select corps of well-trained military police whose organisation, training and discipline came under the direct control of the Ministry of War. It was the senior corps of the regular army. The lowest rank was a corporal, so that Carabinieri would have authority over army conscripts.

The Carabinieri had a dual role: they were the military and field security police of the army, responsible for the registration of the annual conscript classes and the smooth working of mobilisation; they also performed the duties of a civilian police force along with the Corps of Public Security Officers and in larger cities the Municipal Police. Other peacetime functions included attendance at law courts and the providing of guards of honour, escorts and special guards at docks, railways, etc.

In wartime their duties included traffic control, escorting prisoners of war, administration of prisoner-of-war camps, security of lines of communication and base areas, guarding of vulnerable points and supervision of population in occupied areas.

There was also provision for their use as regular combat units as well as a military police force, but only in time of emergency. For this they were organised into combat units no larger than a battalion as a mobile force, to be used for reconnaissance and liaison between operational units.

The Carabinieri were organised as follows: GHQ, Rome; three divisions; one high command of the CCRR – for Albania; seven brigades or zone inspectorates; twenty-three territorial legions; the Central School of CCRR and one Cadet Legion.

In addition, two battalions were attached to the Rome (central Italy) territorial legion and one to the Bolzano (northern Italy) and Palermo (southern Italy) territorial legions. The Rome territorial legion also contained a special squadron of CCRR which formed the king's bodyguard called *corazzieri*. These bodyguards wore crested helmets and armoured breast plates. There was also an independent group of CCRR for the Aegean Islands.

Carabinieri were of two classes, 'effective' and 'auxiliary'. The former normally enlisted for three years, with the idea of making the service their profession. The latter, who may after a year have become 'effective', were men who did the whole or part of their two-year conscript service in the Carabinieri.

A Carabinieri motorcycle column pauses by the roadside during a patrol in northern Italy. (Author's collection)

In addition, regular soldiers were attached to the Carabinieri with the title of 'attached Carabinieri', though only in cases of necessity.

On enlistment, all recruits, except those who had already had at least six months' service in the army, navy or Carabinieri, were sent on a six-month course at the Cadet Legion in Rome.

The Finance Guard was an integral part of the armed forces, with its members recruited largely from mountaineers with an intimate knowledge of the frontier districts. In peacetime it operated under the Ministry of Finance; in wartime it was transferred to the Ministry of War. Finance Guards were stationed along the land and sea frontiers of Italy, and also at important commercial centres throughout the country. Their peacetime functions were the prevention of smuggling, assistance in the collection of taxes, the suppression of attempts at espionage across frontiers and the collection of intelligence reports on adjacent countries.

In wartime the Guard placed all its forces along the land frontiers and the coast at the disposal of the army, and, in co-operation with the Frontier Militia and Frontier Guard, provided a covering core during mobilisation. In addition, it performed certain duties for the navy and assisted in police work, requisition and industrial mobilisation throughout the country while carrying out its normal duties for the Ministry of Finance.

In the Albanian campaign some battalions were formed and used as ordinary combat soldiers, though in general their adequacy for combat duty was limited – even though they had thorough elementary military training – because their armament was not equal to that of a normal infantry battalion. Any use in the field was therefore limited tactically.

Enlistment was for three-year periods until the soldier had completed twenty years' service, after which they could re-enlist for only a year at a time.

Conscripts' Training

In general, conscripts for the various divisions were recruited from their own divisional district, as were army corps from their own corps areas. Alpini Divisions were also invariably conscripted from the mountaineers of their own locality.

Alpino Tullio Lisignoli of the Battaglione Morbegno, 2 Alpini Divisione Tridentina, remembers:

I was conscripted when I was nineteen and my father, who had fought in World War I and who had been wounded several times, said to me, 'Look, you go, but don't be a hero because if you be a hero you won't come back. Try to defend yourself when it is time to defend yourself, but don't be a hero'. I joined my unit for training on 9 January 1941, around the Bolzano and Brennero Pass areas in northern Italy. The soldiers in my regiment were more or less all from the same province I came from, and so we all spoke the same dialect. Being from the same area was, in my view, a good thing, as we were all like brothers and looked after each other. This applied especially during the retreat in Russia.

Blackshirt Antonio D'Angelo:

There were more southern Italians in the army in Ethiopia. This was because southern Italians were much poorer – farmers or unskilled labourers – as opposed to the well-to-do northerners, thus, many joined the army. I recall there was even an all-Sicilian outfit called the 'Divisione Vespri'. Yes, many were Abruzzese, Molinesi, Calabresi, etc. But I recall several comrades in my unit from Trieste, Florence and Torino. This could be a barrier to a minor extent as a soldier from Milano did not mix with a soldier from Sicily.

When the conscripts were called up they were assigned to depot units, each of which equipped and trained them as a regiment. The depot had storehouses for clothing, equipment, arms and vehicles from which the conscripts were issued the necessary uniforms and gear.

When regiments were moved into a theatre of operations, the personnel of the depot commands (which were distinct from those of the field armies) remained at their posts to equip and train other regiments. Depots and their regular regiments had the same numbers. Regiments subsequently trained were given new numbers.

An Autobilinda AB41 armoured car and crew from the Central Instruction School for tank and armoured personnel. (Author's collection)

Divisions and, occasionally, regiments were known by geographical and historical names, sometimes by names of prior military or royal commanders, by nicknames or by a combination of a nickname and a geographical name. For example, 'Lupi di Toscana' – Wolves of Tuscany, or 'Cacciatori Delle Alpi' – Alpine Hunters. Regiments could take the name of their division, or if they had had long service such as the three grenadier regiments of 'Granatieri di Sardegna', were allowed to give their names to the divisions.

The prolonged reorganisation of the Italian army, begun after World War I, resulted in a new concept for its infantry. Manoeuvrability was sacrificed to the development of increased attack capability and the ability to undertake deep penetration of enemy positions. However, in contrast to the German system of selecting first-class personnel for infantry units to make this arm the mainstay of forces in the field, the Italians tended to subordinate infantry to other specialities. This created a pool into which were directed all those soldiers not particularly fitted for one of the more highly regarded branches, such as artillery, armoured units, paratroops or Alpini.

The training of the conscript masses followed a set routine which turned out soldiers of a fixed military standard. It was necessarily limited and rather superficial, but this defect was remedied at least partially by pre-military training, by drastic reduction in exemptions, by post-military training and by frequent recall to duty.

As far as time permitted soldiers were given thorough individual and unit training in combat techniques. Whenever possible they were trained for service in the type of terrain in which they were most likely to serve in the event of war.

General Bastico (second left) confers with General Rommel, in the region of the Got el-Ualeb sector, Libya 1942. (Bundesarchiv, Koblenz)

The aim of unit training was for each unit to reach a level of ability that would enable it to meet the tactical and logistical problems of the battlefield successfully. Special emphasis was placed on mountain warfare, particularly during winter. Great stress was laid on co-operation of the different arms, especially between infantry and artillery for a war of movement.

For the infantry and fast-moving mobile units, the fundamental combat unit was the platoon, at which level training was of the greatest importance. Only when this was perfect was the training of larger units undertaken. Infantry command was greatly decentralised, with platoons and sometimes squads acting largely on their own initiative during offensives.

These theories, for various reasons, did not always equate so well in practice, as the following opinions expressed by Nazi Germany's General Erwin Rommel in 1941 illustrate*:

The Italian soldier is disciplined, sober, an excellent worker and an example to the Germans in preparing dug-in positions. If attacked he reacts well. He lacks, however, a spirit of attack, and above all, proper training. Many operations did not succeed solely because of a lack of co-ordination between artillery and heavy arms fire and the advance of the infantry. The lack of adequate means of supply and service, and the insufficient number of motor vehicles and tanks, is such that during some movements Italian sections arrived at their posts incomplete. Lack of means of transport and service in Italian units is such that, especially in the bigger units, they cannot be maintained as a reserve and one cannot count on their quick intervention.

Generale Ettore Bastico, Italian Commander in Africa, replied to these comments:

The picture drawn by General Rommel about the attitude towards combat of our units is undoubtedly in accord with reality. However, I have had it pointed out to Rommel that the prime reason for this attitude is not a lack of aggressive spirit on the part of our men but a deficiency – both in quality and quantity – in the arms with which they are supplied, in contrast to the power and the quantity of the English armour. Also the poverty of our logistics, arising either out of the organic composition of our units (the only motorised one was the Trento which now has 80 per cent – I repeat 80 per cent – of its vehicles out of action) which just do not have the means necessary for the motorised transport,

*Translation of extracts from Comando Supremo by U. Cavellero 1940–43 Diary. National Archives NZ. File WAII 11,26.

or out of the many difficulties in receiving from the Motherland the means necessary for maintaining and improving their equipment.

Shortages of supplies afforded to Italian soldiers by the often tenuous sea and air link between Italy and Africa, coupled with the comparative deficiencies in their equipment and arms, led to them being subjected to long periods of combat without much chance of relief. One archive report states:

British Command, even in quiet periods, did not keep its units in the front line for more than twelve days and, after that, gave them four days' complete rest in the rear. On the other hand, our soldiers [Italians] had for months not had any relief from front-line duty; rest was almost unknown to them, as was also the system of relieving for home leave units that were tired and worn from many months of exhausting life and combat in the desert.

There were divisions among the soldiers that had been fighting for more than twenty-four months in the front line, and that had greatly exceeded the theoretical 200 days which American and British experts have set as the maximum limit of physical and psychological resistance in battle, after which, according to them, the soldier becomes exhausted and militarily inefficient.

If the Italian soldier, deprived of means and exhausted, has retreated before the superior numbers, strength and buoyant morale organisation of the enemy – if he has retreated it is because the limits of human endurance had been exceeded and he could not do otherwise.

One incident in Tobruk, Libya, during June 1941 must have dealt a particularly damaging blow to the morale of the Italian soldiers concerned. A company of Australian engineers overran an Italian infantry battalion, and approximately 200 men were taken prisoner, disarmed and marched back inside the Tobruk perimeter. Food for the defenders was severely rationed, and they certainly did not need 200 extra mouths to feed. So the Italian prisoners were sent back, into the German lines – after a large circular hole had been cut out of the rear of all the prisoners' trousers!

While the individual initiative of the Italian soldier was not remarkable, it should be noted that he was raised under a system of government which made discipline seem simple and natural. He was tough, hard and able to endure cold, exposure and insufficient food. He was an extremely good worker who could lay aside his arms and do fourteen hours of hard labour a day without complaint.

Sometimes the rule of discipline was taken to extreme measures. Antonio Cioci, Reggimento Giovani Fascisti, recalls:

A great deal of effort was given to the camouflaging of the trenches and weapons, to the point that two soldiers took it literally and were seen coming back, after a patrol, to the trenches pushing a pram. The officer who was following them with field glasses discovered that inside the pram, well covered by little curtains, were the soldiers' rifles and grenades to comply with the order to camouflage all the weapons. There was general laughter, which goes to show that not even the artillery shells could bend the spirit of these young soldiers.

Before World War II there were canteens known as 'the house of the soldier' in which could be bought small goods such as cigarettes, wine and playing cards at discounted prices. These canteens were operated by a Fascist organisation known as National Operation for Afterwork (OND), which also ran leisure-time activities for military personnel.

The OND had special vehicles equipped with movie projectors and sound equipment for showing feature films. These were driven around to different military units and in the evenings movies were screened for their entertainment. During wartime they were shown behind the front lines. There was, however, no official military organisation comparable to the British NAAFI.

In every Italian town there were brothels used by soldiers and civilians alike which were medically supervised by national health authorities. In North Africa, mobile brothels were sent to various Italian units for officers and other ranks. These were initially headquartered at Sidi Barrani and were staffed by Italian girls, with a strong reinforcement of native women. After the Italian retreat of 1941 no more such mobile recreational facilities were used in North Africa, although there were still brothels to be found in the rear areas such as Tripoli and Benghazi.

A New Zealand soldier recalls:

During the pursuit of the Afrika Korps in November 1942 my unit arrived in Sollum, Egypt. We found in one of the damaged buildings twelve Italian prostitutes, one of whom had been wounded in the thigh by a piece of shrapnel.

The girls said they were originally on their way to an Italian headquarters at El Daba before being stranded during the retreat. We patched the wounded girl up and arranged for them to be shipped back to Alexandria in Egypt by sea on a large British transport barge.

Relates Bob 'Hooker' Holt of the 2/3rd Australian

Soldiers relax with a game of cards. August 1941. Sollum, North Africa. (Rudy D'Angelo)

Infantry Battalion, 16th Brigade, 6th Division, 2nd Australian Imperial Force:

A chap by the name of Chester Wilmot had made a worldwide reputation for himself as a war correspondent during the desert campaign and later in the war in Europe. We saw quite a lot of him during the fighting in Bardia and Tobruk in North Africa.

However, he was wide of the mark and gave us a laugh later, when we read the article he had written about the civilian womenfolk being evacuated from Tobruk and, what is more, he had photos to prove it. The true story was a little different. On the first day in Tobruk [20 January 1941] we came across a group of buildings that in reality was a brothel for the garrison [which had swelled to around 27,000 men at that time]. The Italian ladies of easy virtue were lined up with stacks of suitcases and luggage. They were squealing and screaming something awful. A few of us tried to pacify them, but it only made them more hysterical and we moved on and left them to their own devices.

Recalls Blackshirt Antonio D'Angelo:

Our off-duty activities included reading, writing letters, art work, playing cards, taking long walks, singing, dancing and what was called 'field architecture' built everywhere the Italians went. These included small chapels, stone buildings and sculpture. After the war in Ethiopia, during our occupation, some soldiers did have money available for movies, a restaurant or entertainment in towns such as Addis Ababa, Asmara, etc.

The conscript, during the initial eighteen months of service, was allowed ten days' leave. After another eighteen months a further thirty days were allowed. For officers, leave depended on seniority of rank and ranged from twenty up to forty-five days. During wartime leave was not granted automatically: soldiers had to request it. At popular holidays like Christmas or Easter leave was theoretically granted on merit, but in practice depended on whether the officer liked you and whether time was available. Only death or serious illness in the family prompted compassionate leave, and even this had to be requested through the correct channels.

Special leave was often granted to farm workers to enable them to help gather the harvest, especially during the summer, or in September for grape-picking. According to the type of crop it was given for a period of up to one month, and continued to be allowed during wartime.

Warrant Officer and NCO Training

In the Italian Army warrant officers or *Maresciallo* were divided into three grades, while sergeants and sergeant-majors were classed as non-commissioned officers or *Sottufficiali*. These career soldiers were carefully selected and were promoted or eliminated by competitive examination which took account of both ability and seniority. They were trained at special service schools as well as with soldiers.

In wartime all NCOs and the majority of warrant officers came from the ranks of conscript soldiers. Their military education was not as comprehensive as that of the career NCOs and warrant officers.

Sergente Maggiore Luigi Bonechi of Divisione Forli, 36 Reggimento Artiglieria Divisionale, 2 Gruppo Pezzi Sneider 75/27 mod. II, recounts:

In my capacity as Sergeant-Major I feel I had a very thorough training at the NCO School of Artillery in Nocera Inferiore.

The morale of soldiers in my division was high. Many had been recalled to duty, although when war was declared on 10 June 1940, I saw many officers and soldiers cry like babies.

As a soldier, it is my opinion that only Mussolini and his entourage wanted war against France and Greece. They discredited our country – both wars were imperialistic aggressions.

I would like to point out that the Italian people were under the influence of Mussolini's propaganda and were concerned only with work and enjoyment and not war, especially after the two recent wars in Ethiopia and Spain.

I fought the French, with my battery on the Western Alpine Front in the area around Chiappera. We fought duels with the French with we Italians having the worst of it because the French were firing 305 mm shells while the best we could reply with was our 149/39 artillery.

Our uniforms were not suitable for fighting at that altitude. We were sent to fight in summer garb: our boots had cardboard soles, while the greatcoats were not water-proofed. The result was that many soldiers suffered from frostbite.

I would like to relate to you a curious episode which happened when I was transferred to the Greek/Albanian Front after I had fought in France.

One morning I was driving a 25 cwt truck towards the Telepeni Valley, a crossing of great strategic importance. The bottom of the valley was churned into a sticky yellow mud by the continued passage of soldiers, animals and vehicles. In the middle of the valley 500 mules belonging to my division, part of the Julia and Tridentina Alpini Divisions, had been tethered in a circle.

Suddenly there appeared in the sky an RAF Bristol Blenheim bomber, the sort which had been raiding the skies over Albania for several months. Naturally the British pilot did not miss the concentration of mules in a perfect circle.

He leisurely dropped four or five 100 kg bombs, killing 240 mules and wounding 220 more. I attended to the unwounded forty because I specialised in the handling of pack animals. This tragic episode showed to me the point human stupidity could arrive at.

Carabinieri NCOs and warrant officers were appointed from Carabinieri who had attended an eight-month course at the Central Carabinieri School in Florence. Finance Guards with special qualifications were sent for a nine-month course at a school for NCOs at Caserta, in southern Italy, near Naples.

Officers and Their Training

Active (Regular) Officers who started with the rank of second lieutenant, were drawn mainly from graduates of the military academies at Turin (artillery and engineers) and Modena (other arms) in northern Italy; they were officers and warrant officers who had completed a special course for applicants of this class. There was also a certain intake from complementary (reserve) officers who, after completing their ordinary training, decided to adopt the army as a profession.

A corps cadet school was maintained in each of the territorial corps areas. All conscripts with a high school diploma attended one of these schools unless the necessary quota of officers had been filled for that year. Attendance was compulsory: if the conscript ignored this directive he was sent to serve in the ranks. In peacetime an average of 60 per cent of these cadets were rejected and sent to serve in the ranks.

After graduation, and with not less than three months' service with a regiment, cadets could apply for appointment as permanent second lieutenants. Applicants were sent to one of the military colleges – at Rome, Naples or Milan – which were preparatory to the military academies of Turin and Modena. As soon as the regular officers were commissioned, they spent one to two years (according to branch of service) at training school.

Tenente Claudio Andreanelli remembers:

I volunteered and entered the Royal Military Academy in Modena in 1933. My commander at that time was General Italo Garaboldi. I had good training which lasted two years in Modena and two years in Parma at the Application School. I was then commissioned as a second lieutenant in the 17 Fanteria Reggimento, Divisione Acqui. I later transferred to the 50 Fanteria Reggimento, Divisione Parma.

In August 1940 I was sent to summer camp in Val Pusteria in northern Italy, then to Albania by boat and from there to fight in the Koriza province of Greece, where it was winter though we had no winter equipment with us. My training did not prepare me fully for the sort of campaign we fought. It was a war nobody understood, especially the soldiers, who kept asking their officers what it was all about. Before I went to Greece I respected Mussolini, but while there I lost all respect for him.

Youths who attained a certain standard of education were compelled by law to carry out their conscript service as complementary or reserve officers. These soldiers formed the main source from which junior officers were allocated on mobilisation. They did seven months' service as aspirants in 'school units' and the remainder as officers in service units. Subsequently they were liable for a certain amount of post-military training. Conscripts who successfully completed the course in a corps area school could be commissioned as complementary second lieutenants without going to a military academy. However, this led to the reserve officers being poorly trained compared with their regular army counterparts.

Capitano Enrico Buffoni recalls:

I was called to service in January 1940 and was sent to the Infantry Officer Cadet School at Ancona. After six months I graduated with the rank of second lieutenant.

In July 1940 I was transferred to Army Headquarters in Tripoli, Libya, where I was assigned by HQ to a restricted team of a dozen officers who acted as land navigators. I had a practical knowledge of astro-navigation as astronomy was a hobby of mine.

During 1940/41 the Italian army faced a sort of guerrilla war along the borders of Libya in the south. Such operations against the roaming Allied forces called for professional navigation, as you can imagine. Later, in 1941/42, the warfare moved to the well-known grounds of what the British called the Western Desert, and we the Eastern Desert.

So, any time a unit had to move away from the Via Balbia [the coastal road] the commander of the unit would request a guida for staff work. A more rewarding use of navigators was for tactical reconnaissance.

During my time in Africa I came in contact with almost all the Italian divisions operating in the area and after June 1941 I also served with the German Afrika Korps. By the end of 1942, after the battle of El Alamein, I followed the long retreat to the Tunisian border, mostly as a company or battalion commander. My rank rose to captain.

I recall one incident in particular. It was 27 June 1942. After days of confused fighting we (by that I mean the Afrika Korps, including German and Italian units mingled together) were on the outskirts of the Mersa Matruh defences.

Just before dusk we succeeded in getting very close to Matruh railroad station (a small white hut in a shambles). The fighting slowly stopped. It was a beautiful night, and we hoped we would have a chance for some rest and sleep.

But the RAF arrived, in the form of an estimated 300 Flying Fortresses just shipped from the USA to the Egyptian front. We were carpet-bombed, with many bombs and flares dropped upon us.

There were no shelters, and nobody could move around much, so I took my party under six or seven railroad cars

An officer's batman pours a drink for an infantry Major and his guest, a German Luftwaffe officer. April 1942, North Africa. (Bundesarchiv, Koblenz)

standing on the rail line just a few metres from the hut.

We felt quite safe and protected under the wheels of the wagons and eventually succeeded in getting some sleep. At dawn we reluctantly left our shelter, in order to resume the race for the delta.

As soon as there was enough light, I cast a glance at the wagons to read 'High Explosives', 25-pound ammo, anti-tank mines and the like! So we had spent the best part of the night 'protected' by a few hundred tons of explosives against repeated RAF bombing. Actually, a few wagons did bear marks of bomb splinters. The train was probably one of the RAF targets. Who knows?

A report from Generale Bastico, Italian commander in Africa, to Generale Ugo Cavallero in August 1941 outlined his impressions of junior officers:

Divisional commanders were unanimous in informing me that while subalterns, apart from a few exceptions, are rendering good service – even when they come from auxiliary sources, the same cannot be said for the majors and captains recalled from the reserve. These latter in general are too old, and even if they have the will and spirit of

sacrifice they lack energy and the capacity necessary for carrying out their duty. Also, nearly all of them reached their rank by successive promotions, the fruit of very brief periods of service. They were also unanimous in lamenting the fact that these officers, nearly all of them, come unprepared and therefore unsuited for the command of their units, or they suffer from congenital illnesses and after the briefest stay they have to be removed – because of professional incapacity or poor health.

The training of the reserve officers entailed a percentage of the reservoir of them being recalled each year for duty and courses, usually during the summer months. They also underwent theoretical instruction in winter. In normal times the numbers often reached 20,000 to 30,000. Whenever the army was augmented by the recall of previously trained classes, a proportionate number of reserve officers was ordered into active service.

Recruitment of officers in the Carabinieri was on a basis of two-thirds from the military academies and a third from the ranks or by transfer from other branches of the army. All attended a six-month course at the Central Carabinieri School at Florence.

Finance Guard officers were recruited from NCOs and warrant officers of the force not below the rank of *Brigadieri* or over thirty years of age, and from men between the ages of eighteen and twenty-three with secondary school education. Both categories took a three-year course at the school for cadet officers at Rome before appointment.

Officers who served in the colonial forces (in Libya and East Africa) were required to be at least five feet eight inches tall and were chosen from the army, Carabinieri, Finance Guards, civil police or militia. Officers attended a course at the Tivoli Training School before going to the colonies, where service lasted for three years. The colonial forces were commanded by Italians, with natives as NCOs and other ranks.

The military education of officers was, on the whole, considered good, particularly for regulars. Before World War II ineffective officers were weeded out, usually in the lower grades. The War College was an excellent institution for advanced training and, partly as a result of the work there, the general fitness for high command and staff was much improved.

The training for officers was ongoing, all were required to take periodical refresher courses in tactics. Considerable effort was made to impart to individuals the ability to handle soldiers in all phases of combat.

There existed, however – in parts of the Royal Army command in particular – a rather hidebound outlook which at times impeded the operational running of units because of its reluctance to evolve and conform to new concepts often seen as contrary to traditional Italian military procedures.

A telegram to Generale Cavallero from Tenente Colonello Montezemolo in December 1941 outlines remarks made to him by General Rommel during a discussion at the German's command post, which in part said:

There are some excellent commanders; for example those of the 'Savona' (Generale De Giorgis), of the 'Pavia' (Generale Franceschini) and others. But in general the method of command is not suited to this type of war: the commanders lack initiative; they ask for orders on matters that are within their scope to decide almost as if to place the responsibility on their superiors. On the other hand these latter concur in this state of affairs, restricting their subordinates and checking their orders in advance. This leads to stereotyping everything, which is particularly grave in this terrain and with these resources, which demand rapid action and decision.

Rommel's comments touched on the situation as it stood in North Africa, but the problem of command throughout the whole of the Italian army on all fronts went deeper than that. The nature of the Italian Fascist state was such that its achievements were portrayed as superior and free from blemishes; any suggestion to the contrary was construed as an admission of some weakness. This exaggeration of strength blinded the political leaders to the real state of affairs, making them unwilling to admit any fault. This self-delusion was imparted to the higher military commanders, who in turn passed on the methods and weakness of the political system to the armed forces.

However, Fascism did not always enjoy an uncontested place in the hearts of the Italian people. There were also the strong traditional influences of the Church and, to a lesser degree, the monarchy. These institutions restrained many Italians from surrendering themselves unreservedly to the one-party system.

The professional Royal Army officers were mostly royalist in their loyalties, while officers called up for the duration of the war tended to be more pro-Fascist in outlook. Many officers saw through the political posturing and the exaggeration of military might as lauded by Mussolini, but were resigned to the fact that there was little they could do about it. Officers were prepared, however, to do their duty and serve the Motherland to the best of their ability.

Tenente Giuseppe Festa, commander of Mortaio Compagnia, 34 Reggimento Fanteria, Divisione Livorno, comments:

Italy was not prepared for war in 1940, mainly because of the shortage of arms. Mussolini said there were eight million bayonets, but that was a big bluff. However, I supported Italy's entry into the war because I was an Italian officer and that was my duty.

The typical officer had a strong sense of duty towards his country and his men. The nature of the individual Italian is such that he possesses a special, often exaggerated, feeling of honour – although he is also gifted with clear insight into many situations. Even if what he saw was unfavourable he felt compelled to carry out his duties with honour until such time as he deemed it folly to continue.

Every officer was entitled to a batman, who acted as a sort of *aide-de-camp* for delivering messages and orders when required, and provided some personal services such as rigging a tent, preparing meals and the like. Becoming a batman was strictly voluntary and the batman was exempt from camp details and sentry duty.

The discipline administered by officers towards the other ranks was exceptionally strict, the general rule being 'Obey without question!' Officers and men socialised as far as the military code dictated, though officers maintained a professional distance. Outside the confines of the barracks, officers and other ranks very rarely mixed. In the Reggimento Giovani Fascisti, however, former members recall that there was a reciprocal respect between officers and other ranks, as they were all volunteers.

During combat the barriers relaxed somewhat as the question of mutual survival became paramount. Alpino Tullio Lisignoli recounts:

During late December of 1942 my unit was stationed about eighty miles from Stalingrad. The Russians had started a big offensive which broke through our defensive positions and the Germans would not let us move back when the front started to crumble. It was not until we were nearly encircled in late January 1943 that we fell back.

We were all on foot as the motor transport had either run out of fuel or got stuck in the deep snow. There were, however, a number of mules which had been used to carry equipment. These were used to pull sledges made out of whatever could be found to carry the wounded. About eighty per cent of our soldiers had frostbite to the feet, hands or ears.

The leather boots we wore went like steel in the extreme cold, and if a boot was taken off the skin would often come with it. Our woollen socks had either worn out or been lost in the retreat. The only way to stop our feet from becoming frozen was to get a blanket and wrap strips of it around them and then tie them up with wire.

Our equipment was unsuited to the sub-zero conditions. We were supposed to be issued with wool-lined coats, but all we had were grey/green wool capes of the type we wore in Italy. It was not until the retreat that I managed to pick up a heavy wool-lined coat from an army store about to be destroyed by our engineers. The first thing I did when I got the coat was to cut off a strip around the bottom just below the knees and use it to wrap around my head to keep me warm. I threw away my steel helmet as it was useless.

The extra equipment we took with us lasted only three days or so as we couldn't carry it all. We lost all our heavy support weapons, including machine-guns – who was going to bother carrying all the ammunition for them? We did, however, take our rifles and pistols with us. These were essential as every six or seven miles there was a village and we never knew if the Russians would fight us as we passed through.

The big problem was the cold and no food – you had to fend for yourself, find what you could, catch and kill what you could, and eat it raw or with whatever you had.

Many times a soldier would stop and sit down in the snow for a rest and when it was time to move on someone would give him a shake and tell him to get up. But the sitting figure would fall over dead, having died in his sleep. They were left where they fell – the snow soon covered them. Many times I wanted to stop and just give up – it was only the thought of my two-year-old nephew in Italy that kept me going.

During the retreat the officers and soldiers were the same. It did not matter if you were a *generale*. You had to look after yourself. The officers would remove their rank insignia as it made them conspicuous to enemy snipers. Some of the officers killed themselves rather than go on.

My company commander was Tenente Garaboldi, who was the son of Generale Italo Garaboldi, commanding general of our army corps in Russia. I remember the general had sent an aeroplane to collect his son. It was snowing and we could hear a plane circling. We knew it was not Russian by the sound it made. Finally it landed and a pilot got out and asked for General Garaboldi's son, saying he had a plane to take him away. Tenente Garaboldi replied, 'No, I stay here with my men. I won't leave my friends. You put somebody else aboard. The plane left with a wounded soldier, but not Tenente Garaboldi.

We finally reached the railhead at Kharkov after twenty-four days of extreme hardship. Here we stopped and rested while waiting for trains to take us west to Italy. The alarm went up that 'the Russians are coming!' But thankfully it wasn't them, just some Romanian or Hungarian soldiers passing through our lines. Their uniforms were a similar colour to those of the Russians.

That night we were shelled by Russian artillery. The officers tried to get the wounded and sick on to the first train leaving. The rest of us had to walk further up the line. The train with the wounded on board was blown up during a Russian bombardment. I was lucky not to have been one of the wounded.

Chivalry was for the most part swept aside with the advance of modern warfare. However it did still exist, as Tenente Giuseppe Festa remembers:

I was stationed on the Italian/French Alpine Front in July 1940. I was commander of the Mortaio Compagnia, 34 Fanteria Reggimento. It was during the battle of Valtinea. I arrived at a small fort occupied by French soldiers – ten other ranks and an officer, who had just surrendered. The French second lieutenant was wounded, blinded by part of a bomb from our 81 mm mortars. The blind officer wanted to congratulate me, as commander of the soldiers who had shot so very well with the mortar. As he was blind he wanted to touch my hand. A few days later an armistice was declared and the Frenchmen were set free.

System of Promotion for Officers

Promotion took place by seniority up to the rank of colonel, and by selection according to a merit list for the higher ranks.

The system of promotion for reserve officers was clearly prescribed. However, social position sometimes had a good deal to do with an appointment.

During mobilisation, officers for depot and training commands were secured from older officers who were then promoted without examination. This enabled the younger and more active men to be available for combat duties.

A New Zealand soldier recalls:

I was a sniper during the battle of El Alamein in Egypt during 1942. Before sunrise every morning I would go up to the forward observation post with the artillery spotter and would remain in the one position all day. I had orders to shoot officers only.

Looking through my telescopic sight across the distance between our lines I could not pick out the German officers from the German other ranks very easily because of the similarity of their uniforms. With the Italian officers, however, there was never any doubt. Their uniforms looked gaudy to me in comparison to their other ranks. I could also pick out an officer by the exaggerated gesticulations, especially if they had an audience – the higher the rank, the more the hands were waved in the air. I eventually asked for a transfer to the military police because I was a freemason and I was afraid I may have shot some of my brother masons.

Hot rations are issued to an artillery crew in North Africa. (Otto Meyer)

Rations

The Commissariat Service was responsible for the supply and distribution of foodstuffs for the army. Establishments included in the subsistence service of the commissariat were: the military bakeries and mills located with all army corps and most divisions; military hardtack establishments which produced all the hardtack for the army's war needs; military rations depots with all corps and divisions; military port and interior refrigerator plants for storing imported meats; plants for preserved foodstuffs such as tinned meat, soups, condensed broth and sauces in tins; plants for the production of concentrated forage to eliminate foreign oats imported for animals in military service.

In peacetime officers and NCOs had better rations than the other ranks, but these improvements on the standard issue had to be paid for by the recipients. The double standard of rations was a gulf between officers and soldiers.

During World War II rations were theoretically the same for all ranks up to battalion commanders. How closely this order was adhered to depended on the individual unit commanders.

Bersaglieri and Alpini Divisions received extra rations because of the strenuous nature of their deployment. Extra rations were also issued to all soldiers when on the move or on manoeuvres, normally at the end of each march. When local resources were used, soldiers had the task of slaughtering cattle or whatever else was required in the preparation of meals.

The standard meals (called *rancio*) issued to soldiers serving in Italy were usually: breakfast: black coffee, with perhaps two hard bread crackers; lunch: pasta or vegetable soup or rice, meat, bread, fruit and wine (a dixie-full per man); dinner: vegetable soup, pasta, cheese, fruit, wine, tinned beef or beef soup (issued instead of cheese or tinned beef on occasions). The tinned beef was called 'Arabo Morto' (Dead Arab) by soldiers who were issued with it in North Africa, because of the initials AM (Military Administration) stamped on the tins. All soldiers were given a dispensation, known as Papal Permission, which allowed them to eat meat (when available) on Fridays, even Good Friday – 95 per cent of Italians were Catholic and would not normally have been permitted to do this. On Sundays, sweet cakes and sometimes marmalade and chocolate were issued.

Cigarettes were issued to officers and soldiers, depending on supply, once a day. There were various brands available from the Military Administration. One in particular was unpopular with soldiers. Named Milit, the initials were jokingly interpreted as M (*merda*=shit) I (Italian) L (*lavorata*=worked) I (in) T (*tubetti*=little tubes), which didn't say a lot for their quality. Also available from the state-run monopoly were such brands as AOI Three Stars, Serraglio, Macedonia, Savoia and Nazionali Esportazione.

Forces serving outside Italy found their rations varied, depending on the prevailing supply situation. Generally though, the food was much the same as that issued at home, although it was often supplemented with whatever could be obtained from local sources. Blackshirt Antonio D'Angelo recalls:

In North Africa, hot meals were a rarity. We never got them in the combat zone. If there was a rest period from combat, the field kitchen would cut open an oil drum and hunt animals and we would have a hot meal. The bones were used to make soup.

In North Africa some soldiers were issued reserve food, comprising tinned beef and two hard corn biscuits of 200 grammes each. This was only to be rations were sent up to the front line, and only after an order from the battalion commander. Some soldiers also got 'comfort food', which was an extra ration comprising a spoonful of marmalade, 50 grammes of chocolate, a supply of cigarettes, a decilitre of anice and a litre of water per day. Food near the front lines was often eaten cold, as fires might attract enemy attention.

The water ration was laid down as five litres a day per man, although the Italians were able to exist on considerably less than that. Twenty litres a day was allocated for animals.

Cosmo Gaetano, 5 Reggimento d'Armata Artiglieria, recalls:

I was in Albania from February 1942 until September 1943, where my regiment was stationed in Sassolungo.

My friend Galli from Como and myself were on guard duty one day when we became spectators to an Albanian funeral taking place at a nearby cemetery.

Albanians take food instead of flowers to the dead. When the relatives of the deceased had departed we went to the burial ground and stole the food as we were fed up with the usual army rations.

Burials and Graves

The nature of war is such that death is an ever-present reality for soldiers on the battlefield. When casualties

A photographic sequence taken in 1941 at the funeral of an Alpini officer of the 58 Company of the Tridentina Alpine division. Albania. (Author's collection)

occurred the identification and burial of the dead was the responsibility of the Medical Service. However, burial was performed by soldiers of all units whenever it was necessary. Items recovered from the body were firstly the dog tag, followed by all arms and equipment, then any personal effects.

In North Africa it is thought that at least 60 per cent of all Italians killed in action were lost during night patrols, running actions, blown up in lorries or killed in burning tanks in one of the numerous fluid actions that flowed across the desert.

Each regiment had a military priest attached, who usually held a rank between lieutenant and major. The only distinguishing features of the uniform were a special pattern of cap badge (a cross as a central piece surrounded by a wreath and surmounted with a crown for the Royal Army; for the militia a cross super-imposed over a Fascio, sometimes with a wreath and surmounted by a star) and a large red cross covering the left tunic pocket.

During combat the priest comforted the wounded and dying. At the end of an action and in the presence of another officer, he recorded the fallen and compiled a list of personal effects of the dead. The casualty list was sent to the regimental command, which passed it on to the Ministry of War, which communicated the sad news to the next-of-kin.

Alpino Tullio Lisignoli remembers:

Before Christmas in 1942 I was in a reserve position about eight miles from the front line in the Don Basin, Russia. The front had been quiet, with very little fighting for several months.

And so we Italians decided to celebrate the upcoming festive season with a large mass. The weather was so cold it was not practical to have the ceremony outside, so we decided to dig a large underground bunker and hold it there.

We started to dig the hole and after a while some Russian civilians asked us what we were doing, so we told them that we were digging an underground church. The next day there were more Russians than Italians helping with the digging as they wanted to celebrate mass as well, so our officers gave them permission to attend.

The service was conducted by our military priest and was a happy occasion, with Italians and Russians worshipping side by side. Before we were sent to Russia the priests were saying, 'Go serve your country and fight the Bolsheviks as they are against religion.' The civilian population at least was usually co-operative with us Italians, but there was very little love lost between the Russians and the Germans.

Tenente Claudio Andreanelli recalls:

One night in the Koriza province of Greece my orderly went out of the farmhouse where we were sleeping and never came back. Next day I found him sitting on his own 'dirt' with a sniper's bullet hole in his forehead. Naturally I wrote to his family saying he died in combat.

Recounts Blackshirt Antonio D'Angelo:

In combat in Ethiopia there was little time for burial. Often the soldiers who were not quickly buried were eaten within twenty minutes by vultures, crows or other animals and picked 'bone-clean' by these predators. If there was time, the man was buried in a shallow grave not more than a couple of feet deep. This was because in the places where I served the ground was rock hard and it was often impossible to dig any kind of deep hole with our entrenching tools.

When there was time, some casualties were buried in a mass grave. This was usually if we were attacked in our own positions and after the natives had fled. If it was 'on the run' – say in an offensive – we often had to leave the dead on the field. Even when a soldier was buried in a shallow grave, for example, the vultures could smell the decomposing body and would often dig it out and pick it clean, right to the bones.

If a man needed a tunic, pants or boots because his were ripped, worn or needed extensive repair, he often took what he needed off the dead and wore it. When other clothes were left on the body, they were often removed by the natives after burial. Sometimes they even mutilated the bodies.

Soldiers fortunate enough to be buried in a coffin were given a more formal burial, often with honours. Coffins were built by carpenters of the Engineer Corps.

An officer almost always took part in a burial service along with the priest. The officer would unsheath his dagger, raise it in a salute and cry, '*Presente*.' The soldiers present would do likewise. Some officers would cry, '*A noi*' and we would do likewise. It was always a moving experience. Royal Army officers might cry, '*Savoia*,' but it was always the same.

The North African desert could be an eerie, soulful place at night, with the wind howling through the shifting sands. A member of the Reggimento Giovani Fascisti had a 'supernatural encounter' one night when the moon was full. He was standing guard near no man's land at Wadi Zig Zaou on the Mareth Line when he saw something which looked like a ghost. He didn't tell anybody because he didn't want to be laughed at, but a few days later he was again on duty in the same place, and again he saw the white shadow disappearing. This time he fired his rifle, awakening his comrades and incurring the rage of the sergeant, who would not believe his ghost story.

After a long inquest it was discovered that a soldier from the regiment, wrapped in an English parachute against the chill, went to the toilet quite often during the night, creating the vision of a ghost.

All soldiers killed were considered for the next twelve months as 'present with the colours', so their families were assured of some economic recompense. The sum paid depended on the deceased's rank, years of service and the medals he had been awarded.

Epilogue – a New Zealand soldier remembers:

At the end of the war in North Africa in 1943, while on the long trek back from Enfidanville to Egypt somewhere between Tripoli and Benghazi, the brakes on the truck I was driving seized. I had to pull out of our convoy and wait until they cooled off. Feeling a call of nature, I grabbed a shovel and made my way back to a depression.

It was there I discovered a body – an Italian soldier mummified by sand. I found an identity disc on him and a medal. The identity disc was handed in to HQ but I kept the medal. I should say the poor sod was buried where he lay. Through the years I have wondered how he got where he was, as it was miles from anywhere and not by any sort of formed road.

Chapter Two
Army Organisation

Doctrine

THE ITALIAN army had developed a military doctrine called by its General Staff the 'War of Rapid Decision' which to a considerable extent reflected the theory of the German General Staff prior to World War II. Though Italy possessed very limited natural resources, it made efforts to build a large war machine with emphasis on motorisation and mechanisation. The chief features of this policy were: fast-moving divisions, designed for exploitation and reconnaissance; tank brigades, designed for penetration, encirclement and exploitation; and motorised divisions, designed for rapid movement over a wide range and for the reinforcement of mechanised or fast-moving units. Surprise, speed, intensity, sustained action and flexibility of plan allowing for unforeseen contingencies were seen as the basic factors for a successful action.

Soldiers from the Lupi di Toscana infantry division pause for a photograph en route to Albania to reinforce the Greek front. January 1941. (Author's collection)

Italian staff studies and war plans laid very little stress on the defensive, the assumption being that an offensive against its soldiers was a remote possibility. In the colonies of Libya and East Africa any opposition by the native inhabitants was not considered a serious threat and so theories followed those of mainland Italy. Italian military history during World War II demonstrates the inadequacy of a purely offensive war machine, and the Italians, like other armies, found that their main difficulty lay in applying theories rather than evolving them. It was on the 'Rapid Decision' doctrine that army unit organisation was based.

Infantry Divisions

The infantry divisions during World War II were known as 'binary' divisions because they incorporated two infantry regiments; only two divisions of grenadiers still employed the old three-regiment organisation.

From 1 March 1940, a Blackshirt Militia Legion was supposed to be attached to each infantry division, partly to include Blackshirt soldiers with regular army formations and also to increase the number of infantry therein. The legion was intended to act as an independent mobile unit, its men being used as assault soldiers.

One artillery regiment was attached to each infantry division. This was either pack (where the guns were disassembled and secured to the backs of mules in purpose-built packs for transport) or horse-drawn, but certain pack types could be horse- or tractor-drawn.

The wartime establishment strength of an infantry division was: headquarters, two infantry regiments, one artillery regiment, anti-tank company, mortar battalion, pioneer company, signals company, medical section, supply and motor transport sections, and a Blackshirt legion.

The weakness of the binary division became evident during the Greek campaign. Divisions which suffered heavy losses had to be reformed with whatever infantry was available or even by merging with another division.

Truck-Borne Infantry Divisions

There were reportedly two types of truck-borne divisions: 'European' and 'North African'. The European type differed little from the regular infantry division, except that it may have had mechanised artillery, no Blackshirt legion and two divisional mortar battalions in the field.

A 'North African' division comprised two infantry regiments, one artillery regiment, one light tank battalion, one support anti-tank battalion and one engineer battalion.

Although these divisions were theoretically motorised, the motor transport needed to lift a division entirely was not allotted but was drawn as and when required from the Commissariat. The European divisions retained a good proportion of animal transport which enabled them to operate, when grounded, in 'horsed' columns. The animal transport, which could be lifted and transported by rail or motor transport, was sometimes referred to as a 'pack train'.

Mountain Infantry Divisions

These were infantry divisions specially equipped for mountain warfare, they had similar composition to an infantry division, but with additional animal transport and rather more manpower.

The guns of the artillery regiment could all be transported as horse-drawn wagonloads or by pack animals.

Alpini Divisions

These were essentially specialised mountain divisions, with their personnel drawn from Alpine regions. The standard of physique and training was high and the artillerymen were expert in the manhandling of pack artillery. The regiments had their own permanent detachments of artillery, engineers and ancillary services.

The Alpini units had a flexibility of organisation dictated by the difficulty of employing large formations in mountainous conditions. An Alpini division was, therefore, often only an administrative headquarters. In the Greek campaign, regiments operated as independent formations, with a full complement of supporting arms and services. Links between each unit and with parent organisations were usually maintained, however.

A typical Alpini division comprised: headquarters, two Alpini regiments, one Alpini artillery regiment, one mixed engineer battalion, one chemical company, one supply section and one medical section, decentralised to regiments. Detachments fought on all war fronts except North Africa.

Alpini General Santovito and his staff at the forward positions of the 58 company, Tridentina alpine division. Greek/Albanian front, December 1941. (Author's collection)

Mobile (Cavalry) Divisions

These semi-motorised, fast-moving or Celere divisions were designed primarily to carry out the role of cavalry in both manoeuvre and combat. Highly mobile, their main components were two horsed cavalry regiments and one cyclist Bersaglieri (elite infantry) regiment. The cavalry regiments were virtually mounted infantry, while the Bersaglieri soldiers had collapsible bicycles but could also be truck-borne if necessary. The artillery regiment had two motorised and one pack battery, and the division included a support group of light tank squadrons. Fire power was generally sacrificed for a reconnaissance role and as such defence was not one of the great strengths of these divisions.

Three Celere divisions were raised from former cavalry formations. The lack of full mechanisation was found to be a major flaw with these divisions, and though efforts were made to upgrade them, shortages of equipment and trained personnel prevented this from being realised.

War organisation was: headquarters, two cavalry regiments, Bersaglieri cyclist regiment, anti-tank company, light tank group, divisional artillery regiment, mixed engineer company, medical section, supply section and motor group.

Since there were no cavalry divisions in the Italian army, cavalry was primarily employed with the Celere divisions, or attached to other corps as required. In general, the cavalry mission was that of reconnaissance and, in cases of necessity, to exploit advantages gained or close gaps etc. It deployed mounted and fought either mounted or on foot.

Many cavalry depots also formed dismounted squadron groups which were used in coastal or other home defence roles, particularly in southern Italy and the islands. In 1939 the cavalry arm consisted of thirteen regiments of horse and two squadrons of autonomous soldiers, comprising 1.5 per cent of the armed forces.

Italian cavalry officers were generally of the wealthy and socially eminent classes, and horsemanship was more than a military interest. Hence the training of

A squadron of cavalry on patrol in Russia, September 1941. (Rudy D'Angelo)

A Carro Armato L6/40 tows a German Army truck out of difficulties. Armed with a 20mm cannon and an 8mm coaxial machine-gun, it was normally assigned to reconnaissance units. (Bundesarchiv, Koblenz)

cavalry horses was uniformly excellent. In spite of this, ordinary troop horses were of an inferior standard.

The last two cavalry charges made during World War II and possibly in modern times were made by the Italians. The first was in Russia in 1942. The Reggimento Savoia Cavalleria, a heavy dragoon regiment and one of the oldest traditional cavalry regiments (sent to Russia as part of the Italian Expeditionary Corps in support of their German allies, who had already taken part in the battle for Stalingrad and the first defensive battle of the Don), were encamped for the night of 23/24 August in the area between Yagodny and Chebotarevsky, having been sent to halt the enemy advance in that region. Early in the morning a scouting platoon made contact with two Siberian battalions numbering 2000 soldiers, and a fierce exchange of fire ensued.

Heavily outnumbered by the Siberians, the Italian colonel ordered a cavalry charge. In three separate charges the four squadrons of cavalry, numbering 600 men in total, broke through and routed the enemy with a loss to themselves of thirty-nine men and two officers. The Germans who witnessed the charge were incredulous and so impressed that they congratulated the Italians with a citation.

The final charge was on 17 October 1942 by 14 Reggimento Cavalleggeri d'Alessandria, a light cavalry regiment attached to the 1 Divisione Celere Eugenio di Savoia. They were participating in anti-partisan police duties against Tito's army in Yugoslavia in the area of Perjasica, between the rivers Mreznica and Korana.

During the night the Italians were encircled in the woods by part of the 20,000-strong partisan army. The regiment was ordered to retreat towards the nearest village, away from the woods. To comply with this order meant breaking through the enemy lines as an alternative to surrendering.

A break-out was ordered and, under heavy enemy automatic and mortar fire, the cavalry squadrons made repeated charges before a breach in the lines was held, allowing the remaining Italian force to escape.

Armoured Divisions

The original tactical concept of the armoured division was of a mobile reserve to be used in the exploitation of battlefield success or to counter enemy penetration. It was also to engage in reconnaissance with mobile units, wide envelopment of an enemy flank, infiltration

A L3/35 tankette and crew in North Africa, June 1942. Armed with a 6.5mm machine-gun, it was known as the 'Sardine Tin Scout.' (Bundesarchiv, Koblenz)

A medium M11/39 tank in the vicinity of Sidi Barrani, November 1940. (Author's collection)

through gaps or assault against hastily prepared defensive positions.

This cautious conception was modified as a result of the disastrous lessons of early World War II, when a large percentage of tanks used in North Africa in late 1940 and early 1941 consisted of L3 tankettes – little more than light armoured reconnaissance vehicles and no match for the more heavily armoured British Matilda tanks.

This unfortunate state of affairs occurred because hostilities broke out much earlier than Italian military planners had anticipated. As a result they did not have sufficient quantities of medium armoured vehicles (the heaviest class of tank produced by Italy in early 1940 was the M11/39, which weighed eleven tons) immediately available to field against the Allies. The only vehicle which existed in quantity was the L3.

Tactics and training were somewhat rudimentary until the armoured divisions came under German influence and the Nazi tactical doctrines were introduced; Italian armoured forces were then in a continual state of reorganisation as newer equipment and tactics were developed.

A M13/40 tank with two of its four-man crew sitting outside. The lightly armoured turret and front plates are reinforced with spare track. North Africa 1942. (Bundesarchiv, Koblenz)

Bersaglieri astride their motorcycles during summer camp in Italy, 1939. Motorcycles such as these were used for light reconnaissance in motorised divisions. (Author's collection)

Italian armour was organised and trained primarily to operate in conjunction with infantry, motorised or Celere troops. It was not designed to act as a spearhead of the army in the seizure of important objectives or terrain – this task was allocated to the other mobile divisions.

The pre-World War II armoured divisions were a mixture – primarily of L3 tankettes with an equal mix of artillery and infantry. Under German influence they changed radically in composition, with the introduction of medium tanks, self-propelled guns and heavier divisional support weapons. At the beginning of World War II tanks were not fitted with radio, but gradually most became so equipped.

The usual wartime organisation of an armoured division was: headquarters, one tank regiment, one Bersaglieri regiment, one support and anti-tank battalion, one artillery regiment, two 20 mm anti-aircraft batteries (motorised), one mixed engineer battalion, one supply company, one medical company and a gasoline and oil supply platoon.

Italian armour fought on all fronts, although the majority were sent to North Africa. Four armoured divisions were raised: the 131 Centauro was formed on

20 April 1939 and fought in Albania, Greece and Yugoslavia with elements sent to Tunisia at the end of the North African campaign; the remaining units in Italy were disbanded by the Germans in Italy in September 1943. The 132 Ariete was formed on 1 February 1939 and was in North Africa from early 1941 until its virtual destruction as an operational division during the El Alamein battles in November 1942. The 133 Littorio was formed in 1939 and fought on the French Alpine Front, in Yugoslavia, in 1941 and in North Africa until its destruction around El Alamein in November 1942. Surviving elements of the Ariete and Littorio divisions formed part of the Ariete Tactical Group which fought in Tunisia in 1943.

A second Ariete division was formed in Italy as an armoured division. Together with units of the Centauro division it fought briefly against the Germans around Rome after the 8 September 1943 armistice between Italy and the Allies; it was later disbanded by the Germans.

The performance and quality of Italian armoured crews was of a high standard, even when considering the comparative inferiority of their equipment throughout the years of conflict.

Motorised Divisions

Each motorised division was originally formed to work with an armoured division. They also operated with the Celere divisions for strategical reconnaissance or as a general advance guard, often preceded by a light and very fast force of motorcyclists, light tanks or other units on observation missions. There were only two of these divisions, Trento and Trieste, both of which were virtually fully motorised. Their organisation was: divisional HQ, two motorised infantry regiments, one Bersaglieri regiment, one support and anti-tank battalion, artillery regiment, engineer battalion and a services section.

Both divisions fought in North Africa, the Trento from early 1941 until it was virtually destroyed or captured during the November 1942 Battle of El Alamein; the Trieste from late 1941 until the surviving units surrendered in Tunisia in 1943.

Paratroops

The first paratroop school was instituted in Libya in 1938 under orders from Governor Italo Balbo. Located at Castel Benito Airport near Tripoli, it was placed under the control of the Italian Libyan Air Force. The 1 Reggimento Fanti dell'Aria, which comprised Libyan soldiers led by fifty Italian officers and NCOs, was formed from Libyan colonial battalion volunteers. The regiment however, was downgraded to Battalion strength due to the number of fatalities during jump training. It was renamed 1 Battaglione Fanti dell'Aria.

In early 1940 a unit comprising Italian nationals only was formed from Royal Army volunteers. This second force was named the 1 Battaglione Nazionale Paracadutisti della Libia.

In 1941 the 1 Battaglione Fanti dell'Aria took part in the defence of El Fteiah Airport in Libya before withdrawing towards Agedabia where, after hard fighting, it surrendered to British armoured forces.

The 1 Battaglione Nazionale Paracadutisti della Libia was virtually destroyed in early 1941 during fierce fighting against the British Seventh Armoured Division at Beda Fomm, Libya. The survivors were eventually transferred to the Tarquinia Paratroop School in the province of Tuscany to reinforce new

Marshal Emilo De Bono and Governor of Libya Marshal Italo Balbo inspect Libyan Paratroops at Castel Benito, Libya, 1939. (Achille Rastelli)

units being formed there.

In September 1941 the 1 Divisione Paracadutisti was formed and in June 1942 took the name Divisione Paracadutisti Folgore, comprising the 185, 186 and 187 Regiments and the 185 Artillery Regiment.

The original plan was for the division to take part in the occupation of the Mediterranean island of Malta in an operation codenamed C3. But with General Erwin Rommel's successful offensive in May/June leading to an advance into Egypt, the regiments were sent there to fight as infantry and all but wiped out by overwhelming odds at El Alamein in 1942.

The survivors were reorganised into the 285 Folgore Battalion and another independent company, and were all attached to the Trieste Division. The dwindling Battaglione Folgore fought on until it was finally destroyed at the Takrouna stronghold in Tunisia in 1943 towards the end of the North Africa campaign.

In September 1942 the 185 Folgore Regiment, which had remained in Italy, transferred two battalions to the 187 Regiment and was renamed the 185 Reggimento Fanteria Paracadutisti Nembo. The regiment became the core of the new Divisione Paracadutisti Nembo, formed in November 1942 and consisting of the 183, 184 and 185 Regiments and the 184 Artillery Regiment.

The 185 Regiment was sent to the province of Venezia-Giulia in north-eastern Italy in April 1943 to engage the encroaching Slav partisan threat from neighbouring Yugoslavia. Three months later it helped oppose Allied landing forces in Sicily. The remainder of the division was used to defend the province of Tuscany and, from June 1943, the island of Sardinia against an expected Allied invasion force.

A Carabinieri paratroop battalion was formed in 1940. Known as the 1 Battaglione Carabinieri Paracadutisti, it was sent to North Africa in July 1941, where it was intended to be dropped behind enemy lines, but it was used instead to protect the withdrawal of the Ariete division. In subsequent actions it suffered severe losses and was disbanded, the survivors being sent to the 285 Folgore Battalion.

In 1942 an army commando unit based on the British model was raised. Called the X Reggimento Arditi, it was composed of two battalions, each of which had a para company, a frogman (later marine) company and a motorised company. The regiment came under the direct control of the Army General Staff.

Commandos from the X Arditi were dropped to hit various North Africa targets in enemy-held Libya, Tunisia and Algeria and later into occupied Sicily. However, the results of their covert missions were for the most part disappointing, ending in the capture of virtually all men before any real damage could be inflicted.

Field Artillery

The tactical employment of field artillery as laid down in Italian regulations emphasised the following:

(1) Prompt intervention in response to tactical necessities.
(2) Close co-operation with other arms.
(3) Violent action in mass and by surprise.
(4) Co-ordination of the action of the various artillery echelons in order that the effects of fire produce the total results desired in the general concept of the battle, with a single final purpose – that of facilitating the action of infantry.
(5) Elasticity of organisation permitting not only the manoeuvring of fire rapidly, but also the following of the action and its support with the movement of the batteries, particularly when it assumes a character of velocity.
(6) Artillery is useful only if the ammunition supply is assured.
(7) Observation is essential for artillery.

The last-mentioned principle was possibly the most important, for to achieve observation at all times Italian artillery was often situated very forward and resorted to direct laying far more frequently than other armed forces did.

Artillery personnel earned a reputation for good shooting and displayed considerable courage under heavy fire or direct attack. In many cases firing over open sights was used against attacking tanks or infantry.

The artillery arm was spread throughout the army and was classified as divisional, corps and army. These roughly correspond to field, medium and heavy, respectively. There also existed *ad hoc* formations known as *raggruppamenti* (tactical organisations of flexible size and mission) which had no fixed establishment. The artillery manned all mobile anti-aircraft units.

Italian artillery was deficient by the standards of other countries. Notable weaknesses were the retention of obsolete types of both home and foreign (mainly Austrian) makes of weapons. It must, however, be remembered that obsolete weapons were not necessar-

Two artillery soldiers man a captured 'cruiser' tank which has been dug into a fixed gun position. June 1941, North Africa. (Bundesarchiv, Koblenz)

ily ineffective and that in many parts of Italy pack or horse-drawn artillery was more suitable than mechanised forms.

Improvement was slow because of the low technical capacity of the Italian arms industry, and the shortage of artillery was a factor in limiting expansion of the army. All corps and army artillery was motorised. The artillery of the ordinary infantry division was either pack or horse-drawn.

Engineers

Under Italian military doctrine, engineers were considered as technical rather than combat soldiers. An engineer's function was conventional: work on lines of communication, erection and clearance of obstacles, laying of minefields, provision of water, and supply of engineering materials. The providing of signal communications was also an engineering function.

In peacetime the structure consisted of an Inspectorate of Engineers, eighteen engineer corps headquarters, eighteen engineer corps regiments, two mining regiments, two pontoon regiments, one railway regiment, two workshop units and twenty-nine lofts (for carrier pigeons).

There were many types of engineer units in the army's war establishment. They included those which had a combined engineer and communication function, bridging companies, pontoon battalions, an aerial ropeway battalion, a balloonist section, a camouflage company, an electrical mechanics company, a fire-fighting company, a mining battalion, a photographic company, searchlight operators and a water supply company.

There were also assault pioneers known as *guastatori* (destroyers) who were organised into battalions. These 'shock units' nearly always carried out their attacks at dawn, the objective having been approached during the night. They were also known to have been used against tanks at night. These soldiers did not lay mines but were trained in removing them should they impede their progress.

An Assault Engineer School was located at Civitavecchia in central Italy. Instituted at the end of March 1940, it was organised by a Colonel Steiner of the German army.

Signal Corps

The signal service was part of the engineers, there being no signal corps as such. The Italians depended a great deal on radios for communication, even between headquarters and higher authorities. Other means were: optical, by phototelegraph apparatus, signal guns, signal flags and carrier pigeons.

Chemical Troops

A total unpreparedness for gas warfare in World War I, which resulted in many thousands of deaths and casualties, prompted the Italians to establish a Military Chemical Service in July 1923. Serving the navy and air force as well as the army, the service was responsible for chemical warfare in all its forms.

The headquarters were in Rome, where a research and experimental centre was located. Research activities were also carried out in the Universities of Florence and Naples, with an experimental station of the Engineer Corps in Pavia in the north of Italy and gas studies being undertaken at Scanzano Belfiore in the central region.

The peacetime organisation of chemical troops consisted of the Chemical Regiment and a number of separate chemical companies and platoons assigned to army corps and divisions as required. There was a headquarters, a chemical battalion, a mixed chemical battalion, a flame-throwing battalion and chemical depot.

The nucleus of the war organisation was the Mixed Chemical Group assigned to CHQ, which had the following organisation: Nebbiogeni chemical battalion, flame-throwing battalions and a chemical mortar group. The Alpini had a divisional chemical company, which carried larger stocks of mustard gas and chemical mines than the ordinary chemical company. Flame throwers were used extensively by chemical soldiers, who were employed for non-toxic smoke generation duties as well as for toxic gas contamination in its various forms.

A number of different means were employed to disperse the gases. These included the 81 mm chemical mortar – the basic weapon of the chemical troops – smoke and chemical shells for artillery, toxic smoke candles, lacrimatory candles, smoke candles and smoke and incendiary grenades. There was also bulk contamination apparatus and knapsack sprayers, hand-cart sprayers, truck-borne spray apparatus, and light

Signalmen attached to an underground desert radio communication station take a break above the ground. North Africa 1941. (Author's collection)

Members of the 20 Chemical Company in full protective clothing sit aboard a Fiat SPA 38R light truck during a parade in Tripoli, Libya, North Africa. (Rudy D'Angelo)

tank-towed trailers with perforated piping for emission. Principal agents in Italy's chemical arsenal were mustard gas, phosgene, chlorpicrin and arsenical smoke, with tear gas being used in combination with the toxic gases. The Italian chemical industry was quite well developed, although a shortage of coal, coal tar products, chlorine, arsenic, bromine and fluorides limited output.

In the Ethiopian campaign between 22 December 1935 and 19 January 1936, Maresciallo Badoglio reportedly authorised – after permission had been obtained from Mussolini – the use of 200 tons of mustard gas in airburst aircraft bombs. Generale Graziani later used the same method to quell rebel tribes which refused to surrender after the Italian occupation.

Among chemical warfare stores reported found in Libya were drums of mustard gas, but none of the others mentioned previously. The Greeks, however, reported the capture in December 1940 of drums of blister gas, whose composition was approximately equal parts by weight of mustard gas and phenyldichlorarsine. The only time toxic gas was actually known to be used, however, was in Ethiopia.

Frontier Guard

The Frontier Guard was responsible for the fortress duties previously carried out by army corps stationed in frontier districts. In 1939 the Guard was formed into a special corps. Its task remained the defence of frontier districts; but whereas it formerly used only fortress artillery, the re-organisation gained it supporting arms, independence of action, and the primary function of acting as a covering force.

Frontier Guard headquarters were attached to the HQ of the XI Army Corps. Units were allotted a length of frontier divided into sectors, which were further divided into sub-sectors containing a varying number of fortified positions.

Personnel were provided mainly by the army corps, but infantry soldiers were also drawn from the Frontier Guard Infantry Regiment. The regiments and *raggruppamenti* of Frontier Guard artillery were under command of army corps Frontier Guard headquarters and reinforced as required by the artillery units permanently allotted to sectors and sub-sectors.

The Frontier Guard consisted of the following components: eleven Frontier Guard commands, commanded by a Brigade General assigned to headquarters of the corps areas touching the Alpine frontier; a varying number of covering sectors; one Frontier Guard infantry regiment for training and replacements; nine Frontier Guard artillery regiments and one independent Frontier Guard Group.

Each covering sector included a varying number of sub-sectors and minor units of the various arms and specialities, including infantry, artillery and engineers. As a rule, each sector had a depot and the strength of the command varied with the requirements of the particular frontier.

The Militias

The Fascist Militia, popularly known as the Blackshirts, was a purely Fascist organisation which originated from the groups of *squadristi* who had been instrumental in Mussolini's rise to power. In 1923, Mussolini declared the Militia an integral part of the armed forces of the state, while retaining its identity as an independent force.

Officially called the Milizia Volontaria per la Sicurezza Nazionale (Volunteer Militia for National Security) or MVSN for short, it was an independent army and as such was looked upon with deep suspicion and hostility by the Royal Army, a distrust which was never receded throughout the period of the Militia's existence. The Militia was seen as a rival to the Royal Army's monopoly as protector of the state and monarchy.

The formation of the Fascist Militia meant the dissolving of the *squadristi* and as such was opposed by some *squadristi* leaders who had grown rich through their positions of power.

The primary function of the Militia was political, involving the defence and strengthening of the regime (in the Fascists' favour). It was also entrusted with important police duties, mainly in government services at home and in the colonies. Its main military tasks were raising of combatant Blackshirt battalions for service with Royal Army divisions; provision of personnel – for anti-aircraft defence (except in field formations) and coast defence; post-military training; and training of complement officers in the universities.

The organisation of the Militia was directed from the GHQ in Rome by Mussolini, who was commanding general, although the actual day-to-day running was carried out by a Chief of Staff as the executive commander. In wartime the latter came under the direct orders of the Chief of the General Staff. The militia was organised as follows: fourteen zone commands (roughly corresponding to army corps areas of the Royal Army); thirty-three groups of legions; 133 legions; and several autonomous cohorts and detachments. (A legion corresponded in size to an army regiment and a cohort to a battalion.)

A certain overlapping of command existed within the army divisions because of the incorporation into the Royal Army of Blackshirt Militia battalions on the basis of one combat legion to each division. Many of the administrative details of the Blackshirts – such as rank, promotion and assignment of personnel – were dealt with by the Fascist Militia headquarters rather than by the Ministry of War.

Mussolini first announced that Blackshirt combat soldiers would be incorporated into the Royal Army in October 1939. The War Ministry was reluctant to take action or even to discuss their ultimate use as soldiers and, in April 1940, Il Duce learned his instructions were being passively resisted. He immediately issued peremptory orders that his original intent be followed through and the process was subsequently carried out. However, the absorption was not completed until late in 1942 – and only then as a result of a critical need for military manpower.

There were also separate divisions raised which comprised only Blackshirt soldiers, including seven for the Ethiopian campaign of 1935-36. Four new divisions to replace these were formed in 1939 for service in North Africa; they were named 'Libyan' Blackshirt divisions. One of these, the 21 Aprile Division, was disbanded and absorbed into the other three divisions in May 1940. The three divisions were destroyed during the first eight weeks of desert warfare in North Africa: the 3 Gennaio Division was surrounded and captured at Sidi Barrani, Egypt on 12 December 1940; the 23 Marzo and 28 Ottobre were trapped and captured in Bardia on 4 January 1941.

Colonial Militia

In 1924 two permanent colonial legions were instituted in Libya from Italian colonists and volunteers from Italy. These were 1 Legion Oea, based in Tripoli, and 2 Legion Berenice in Benghazi. The Berenice took part in military operations against Arab rebels in Cyrenaica until the latter were finally subdued in 1931.

In 1934 the legions were reduced in strength to cohorts, which in 1935 were redesignated battalions and absorbed into infantry regiments of the Royal Colonial Army.

In each of the Libyan towns of Tripoli, Misurata, Benghazi and Derna, legions were formed and numbered one to four respectively. All four took part in fighting on the North Africa front during World War II and suffered the fate of virtually all the Fascist Militia units there – destruction or capture.

After the occupation of Ethiopia in 1936 seven territorial legions were formed in Italian East Africa. In Ethiopia, 1 Legion was stationed in Addis Ababa, 3 Legion in Gondar, 6 Legion in Gimma and 7 Legion in Dessie; in Eritrea, 2 Legion in Asmara and 4 Legion in Massawa; in Somalia, 5 Legion in Mogadishu. All seven groups were lost during 1941, when a mixed force of British, South African, Indian, Rhodesian, Free French and Belgian troops advanced into Italian territory and, after months of hard fighting (called by the South Africans 'The War of Hundred Days'), eventually defeated the Italian forces.

The Commander in Chief of the Italian forces was Amadeo, Duke of Aosta, a cousin of King Vittorio Emanuele. Mussolini did not hold the duke in high regard, believing that he lacked both military ability and ruthlessness. Although Aosta surrendered at Amba Alagi on 16 May and died as a POW in Kenya in 1942, the campaign did not end until the fall of Gondar in November 1941, thus eclipsing the Italian dream of a 'place in the sun'.

Fascist Albanian Militia

The Fascist Albanian Militia was instituted in September 1939 after Italy's occupation of that country. Four legions were eventually formed from volunteers – the officers were Italian while the NCOs were either Italian or Albanian. The Albanian NCOs were called *Shqipetari*, or 'The Eagle's Sons'. The Militia were stationed in Tirana, 1 Legion; Coritza, 2 Legion; Valona, 3 Legion and Scutari, 4 Legion. All were dissolved in 1943.

Railway Militia

Instituted in 1923, its peacetime duties were the

Blackshirts of the 23 Marzo and 28 Ottobre divisions are among this column of prisoners, part of the 38,000 Italians captured during the attack on Bardia, Libya, by allied forces in December 1940. (Author's collection)

Members of the Coast Defence Militia undergo battery fire control equipment training supervised by two German Luftwaffe personnel (left front). (Author's collection)

maintenance of order and punctuality of the railways, the prevention of fraud and theft, and the discharge of the railway police duties. During wartime they were used as railway protection soldiers. Personnel were drawn from the staff of the State Railways; members could enlist for permanent service or for specified periods. The organisation consisted of an HQ, fourteen legions and forty-nine cohorts, and functioned under the Ministry of Communications.

Port Militia

This militia was instituted in 1924 and charged with police and guard duties in all the principal ports of Italy and its colonies, as well as such coastal sections where a service was deemed necessary. The organisation consisted of an HQ and four legions and also functioned under the Ministry of Communications.

Post and Telegraph Militia

This body was instituted in 1925 and safeguarded the

financial interests of the state by preventing fraud and other dishonesty in the postal, telegraph and telephone services. In wartime it formed the nucleus of the military censorship department and the Field Postal Service. Personnel were drawn from officials and employees of the postal, telegraph and telephone services. It was organised into twenty-seven detachments and it too functioned under the Ministry of Communications.

Forestry Militia

Instituted in 1926, this existed for the protection and exploitation of forests, fisheries and game. Some detachments were given military training and several served as combat soldiers in the Ethiopian and Greek campaigns. The Forestry Militia co-operated with the army over supplies of timber and was employed in the preparation of camp and bivouac sites, water arrangements, etc. The organisation consisted of an HQ, nine territorial legions, one Libyan, Albanian and East African Legion, a motorised legion, three independent cohorts, the Academy of Forestry Militia, and a school for NCOs and other ranks. It functioned under the Ministry of Agriculture and Forests.

Highway Militia

This unit, instituted in 1928, was responsible for road police duties. In time of war it co-operated with the Carabinieri in traffic control and performed special services assigned it by the HQ of the General Staff Corps. It consisted of an HQ in Rome, four group command detachments, seventeen command detachments and three autonomous detachments, with another in Albania. It functioned under the Ministry of Public Works.

Anti-Aircraft and Coast Defence Militia

Although these two militias were administered from a single HQ, their formations were normally separate. During conflict, units of both operated under the control of the local territorial defence headquarters. Personnel were drawn from men aged between eighteen and twenty, those over twenty-seven or unfit for active service, and those living in the vicinity of the batteries. A small cadre of officers, NCOs and specialists were on permanent assignment to the units. A lieutenant-general of the militia commanded both bodies.

Anti-Aircraft was instituted in 1927. The AA defences of the army and of the country itself were separate organisations, the Anti-Aircraft Militia being responsible only for the latter. It manned fixed AA defences, as opposed to the mobile units operated by the army. The organisation consisted of sixteen territorial defence commands, five groups of legions, with twenty-two legions in total, and a central AA Militia School. It also provided personnel for searchlight units and the Observation Service.

Coast Defence, instituted in 1932, was responsible for manning coastal batteries and functioned under the General Staff of the navy. Its organisation consisted of an HQ, two groups of legions, fourteen legions and a school. (Coast defence batteries of defended ports and bases were for the most part manned by naval personnel.)

University Militia

Instituted in 1931 this body was roughly comparable to the Reserve Officers' Training Corps in the United States. It was composed entirely of university students who had reached the age of eighteen; members normally became complement officers on leaving the service. Its organisation consisted of an HQ under an Inspector-General in Rome, nine legions and eighteen independent cohorts for administration; and sixty-nine school detachments, organised by battalions, companies and platoons for training with a detachment based in Libya and Ethiopia. A cohort of the University Militia fought in Ethiopia and some members served in the Spanish Civil War.

Frontier Militia

Instituted in 1927, this was made up of 'special detachments' of the ordinary militia legion located in the vicinity of the frontier. It co-operated with the Public Security Police (the uniformed police force of the Interior Ministry which co-existed in an awkward dualistic system with the Carabinieri) in guarding frontiers against illegal border crossings. It also worked with the Finance Guard in the suppression of smuggling, and with the Royal Carabinieri in making investigations. The organisation consisted of an HQ, a school and four legions.*

Support Services

Commissariat Service

In the Italian army the Commissariat Service performed the functions of the quartermaster corps, except for transportation. It distributed supplies in bulk to the tactical organisations, where storage and issue were handled by line soldiers. The provision of rations, forage, clothing, equipment, barracks and fuel, and the removal and recovery of these materials when damaged or unserviceable, was also under the Commissariat jurisdiction.

Administration Service

All army finances were handled by this service, which

*After 20 turbulent years the Fascist Militias ceased to exist as an entity on 6 December 1943, although the dissolution had begun on 25 July that year, when Mussolini was arrested by the Carabinieri on the king's orders. Royal Army generals subsequently occupied all the Militia's top positions, Royal Army units merged with the MVSN units, and Fascist regalia and titles disappeared from sight. The Fascist Militias were reformed in part as the Republican National Guard during the short-lived northern Italian republic headed by Mussolini from 1943–5.

was responsible for the administration and accounts of higher formations and military establishments. It was constituted to overcome the inconvenience of treating units in the field as administratively dependent on their territorial depots; to relieve the Commissariat Service of the responsibility of accounts; and to control expenditure. In addition to directing and co-ordinating the administration, pay and expenditure of all mobilised units, it also kept soldiers' civil and criminal records.

Transport Service

Charged with the transportation of soldiers and material, this service was sub-divided into rail and water transport, air transport and ordinary transport. The latter included transport by motor vehicle, wagon, pack animal and cable railway.

Rail and water transport was controlled by GHQ through the Directorate of Rail and Water Transport, the territorial executive units being military commands at railway stations, embarkation officers at ports, military ticket offices and the Railway Regiment of Engineers.

The service controlled the country's rail links and the means for river, canal and sea navigation as required by the Ministry of Communications, in accordance with military demands. The maintenance and improvement of rail and water communications and the erection of military field railways were also part of its responsibilities.

Air Transport Service had the responsibility of carrying personnel, material and stores and of evacuating casualties. In practice, it was very loosely organised.

Ordinary Transport Service was responsible for the transportation of soldiers, services and material. It directed the co-ordination of all means of transport, including rail and water, and organised the trans-shipment and unloading of material.

Mechanical transport was provided by the Motor Transport Corps, which included motor transport centres, consisting of headquarters, a depot and a stores office. One centre was assigned to each corps. A variable number of motor transport groups, comprising two or more companies, were in turn divided into three or four motor transport sections – light or heavy – each of twenty-four vehicles.

The Transport Service also provided for road organisation and discipline by means of road movement battalions and light aid detachments assigned to the various armies.

A damaged truck returned home from the Greek front for repair at a motor transport workshop near Bologna in 1941. (Author's collection)

The MT assigned by establishment to units was for the transport of material. Extra MT needed to move soldiers was supplied – in the case of motorised, mobile and armoured divisions – from the divisional MT detachment or group.

In calculating the MT equipment needed to move a given unit or formation, it was estimated the material-carrying trucks would each in addition carry five men. Pack animals were carried in heavy trucks, with two-axled trailers attached, at the rate of four to five animals per truck. Trucks carried an average of twenty-five men. The total MT required to move an infantry division in Europe was estimated to be around 1250 vehicles.

Automobile Service

This service provided for the supply, technical care, repair and evacuation of motor transport by forward mobile workshops and fixed workshops on the line of communications established by the army vehicle park.

Gasoline and oil was supplied from central depots to army vehicle parks and from these to the divisional fuel and oil unit. Enough fuel was provided to allow each type of vehicle or formation to travel 50 kilometres.

Medical Service

This group was responsible for enforcing the rules of hygiene and prophylaxis and for the protection of soldiers from epidemic and infective diseases. It supplied sanitary and medical material, took care of their removal from battle zones and also handled the evacuation and treatment of the sick and wounded, the identification of the dead, and burials.

The surgical facilities and treatment in military hospitals were of a high standard. While army dental treatment was on the whole good, it was somewhat primitive in the sense that a bad tooth was not drilled and filled but taken out regardless. However, dentists were careful about how many teeth were extracted, as a soldier who lost too many could be discharged from service. False teeth for the conscripts were almost unknown in Italy at the time.

The General Directorate for the Military Medical Service was part of the Ministry of War. It controlled the following technical bodies: Board of Legal Medicine, for medical legal advice; scientific laboratories, which carried out research and experimentation in all medical and surgical fields; and the Military Chemical Pharmaceutical Institute, which provided the supply of medicines and medical material for the army, navy and air force.

Army corps directorates supervised the organisation and functioning of the Medical Service in the territorial zone assigned to the corps, in compliance with orders received from higher authority.

The Medical Section inside combat units was an integral part of the divisional organisation and comprised a headquarters, a vehicle detachment, a pack detachment and a stretcher-bearer detachment. An Alpini regiment had a medical section consisting of headquarters and pack and bearer detachments.

Other medical establishments were:

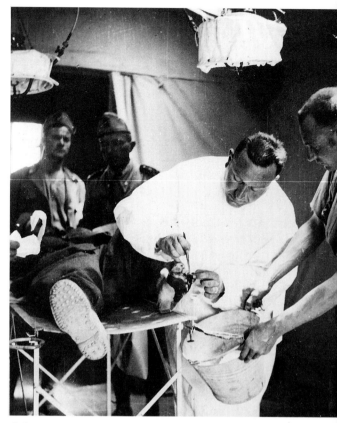

A doctor operates on a wounded soldier in a field hospital in the region of Marmarica, Libya, June 1941. (Rudy D'Angelo)

(1) Casualty clearing stations: designed for assessing the wounded and getting them to field hospitals for initial treatment. They were established under the corps Medical Directorate.

(2) Field hospitals: allotted as required to corps, divisions and Alpini regiments, under the orders of the Army Medical Directorate. The standard field hospital was designed for fifty beds, but could be enlarged to a hundred. It had no transport of its own – this was provided by the army when required.

(3) Specialist ambulances and certain specialised field hospitals in the rear areas were established as required. The specialist ambulances for X-ray and dental treatment were attached to corps field hospitals. Surgical ambulances were attached to armies as available. Field hospitals for infectious diseases or other specialist treatment were organised with appropriately trained medical personnel as and when required.

(4) Base hospitals situated within the war zone: army

medical depots kept the forward medical units and formations supplied with the necessary medical stores.

(5) A disinfecting section was attached to each corps. Decontamination sections were under the Army Medical Directorate, and were allotted to formations as required. They dealt primarily with gas casualties but were also available for providing that rarity at the front line, an ordinary bath.

(6) A chemical laboratory was allocated to each corps and a chemical-bacteriological-toxicological laboratory to each army.

During combat, doctors assigned to units organised first-aid posts (as a rule one to each battalion) close to the line of combat, but well protected. Wounded men were carried to the post by members of the medical corps assigned to the unit.

The medical section was located at points chosen by division headquarters, which took into consideration the front it occupied, the intensity of the action, the proximity to first-aid posts, communication and, finally, the protection provided. The medical section had to be in close communication with first-aid posts and was responsible for the transportation of the wounded from these posts to hospital. Transportation to field hospitals (organised by corps HQ) was entrusted to the medical section with its own motor ambulances.

While an action was in progress, the medical section had to follow right behind the advancing soldiers. All wounded were evacuated to the rear, except those too badly hurt to be transported. These remained with a small group of medical officers and men, while the main body of the section advanced.

In the case of withdrawal, the medical section transported to the rear those wounded who could be moved, leaving behind any who could not with the necessary personnel and material. Soldiers not included in the division were cared for by the medical section or field hospital closest to the area they fought.

The surgical units assigned to each corps were sent to the medical sections of the divisions whenever necessary. Field hospitals assigned to armies or corps could, in a case of absolute necessity, be assigned temporarily to divisions. They were erected in locations well protected against enemy fire, but if possible existing buildings were used. When advanced hospitals were full, unit medical officers would notify the medical director of their army, who would either move wounded to hospitals at the rear or assign additional field hospitals.

In the case of an advance, field hospitals would not be moved, but would be assigned to the last rear unit in the zone of operations. This unit, in turn, would give field hospitals not yet used to the advancing units.

Italian medical units were professionally equal to medical services in either the German or the Allied armies, and the Italian medical personnel were held in high regard by the Germans. Many German and Allied wounded owe their lives to the care and treatment they received from Italian medical units.

Veterinary Service

This service was responsible for the supervision of animal health and the prevention of disease; the collection, evacuation and treatment of wounded and sick animals; ensuring the good quality of meat on the hoof and forage intended for distribution to the troops and animals; and the provision of veterinary and farrier equipment and stores. The Remount Service provided centres outfitting horses and mules.

The service had an inspectorate at the Ministry of War, zone inspectors, and offices with corps and divisions. Its representatives were also located at formation headquarters and with units. It was entirely independent of the Medical Service. Mounted troops had veterinary infirmaries in each regiment.

The specific duties of the directive organisations were: to issue instructions of hygiene and prophylaxis and their enforcement; to ensure army animals were not infected by sick animals belonging to the civilian population; to isolate sick and wounded animals, take care of their treatment if possible or send them to hospitals designated by higher authority; to issue instructions for the killing of animals no longer suitable for service; to supply materials for veterinary services and horse-shoeing; to ascertain the quality of meat and forage; to forward requests for personnel and recommend officers for assignment; and to inspect the veterinary section within the unit.

The Remount Service administered six remount centres (five for cavalry and one for artillery) and three remount squadrons which trained horses between the ages of two and four years. Officers of cavalry and artillery units were attached to those centres. Horse-breeding depots comprised another service administered by the Ministry of Agriculture and Fisheries.

Sick and wounded animals were visited daily by veterinary officers and if none was attached to the unit, animals were either sent to the nearest unit with veterinary staff or a request for a visit was made. When troops remained stationary, animals were assembled in temporary infirmaries if necessary. When the unit moved on sick animals were taken to corps and army infirmaries, which also handled cases requiring longer treatment. Special isolated infirmaries were organised in the case of epidemic diseases. After treatment animals were either returned to their units or sent to the army depot.

The Italian army retained a large number of horses and mules for the transportation of equipment and supplies during World War II (as did the German army). The care and treatment of these animals was therefore of major importance, even in the age of mechanisation.

Obvious similarities in the uniform of a militia captain (left) and a Bersaglieri second lieutenant are well illustrated here. (Author's collection)

Chapter Three
Combat Uniforms

I T IS THE strict duty of a soldier to take care of and wear the uniform in the prescribed order, because he who is seen in public with altered items, or an unclean or untidy uniform, shows not only that he is not well disciplined, but also does not appreciate the military uniform and so does not deserve to wear it.
– Part of standing instructions contained in soldiers' individual record book.

The military clothing and equipment establishment of the Commissariat Service studied uniforms and uniform models for distribution to military factories and regimental tailors, and was also responsible for the manufacture of shoes for soldiers. There also existed central military depots for testing and distributing all regimental material required for clothing and equipment stocks. Headquarters of large units could, if required, authorise the requisition and purchase of linen, shoes and other materials from local sources. Only in special cases were smaller units authorised to secure material.

Military salvage depots were located with army corps and divisions and at all garrisons. They supervised the salvage of old uniforms and equipment, and undertook their disinfection, cleaning and repairs.

Each battalion or regimental command usually had a

The modern-looking open collar tunics worn by the two Militia officers on the left contrasts with the closed collar tunic and kepi worn by the Royal Army artillery officer on the right. The Royal Army was to adopt the open collar tunic in 1933. (Author's collection)

group of tailors, cobblers and barbers who, when drafted, had been engaged to carry on their civilian occupations in the armed forces. There was no special section as such, so repairs and alterations were often carried out by these soldiers. This saved having to send uniforms and the like back to the factory for repair. Just as well, perhaps, as troops joked that if a uniform was sent there for repair the owner usually received it back on the day of his discharge. Also, soldiers in the front line often did not have time to send items away and so carried out repairs on the spot.

Although the Royal Army and the units of the Fascist Militia were separate organisations, items of uniform were standard to both. Apart from some minor detail of garb or insignia particular to certain units, it was often hard at first glance to tell them apart.

In June 1940 orders were issued to both the army and the MVSN, instructing all ranks to wear the same style of uniform, although with their own particular rank and insignia retained. This made the distinction between the two even less pronounced, and as the war progressed the Militia relied even more on the army for supplies, blurring the difference yet further.

Continental Uniforms

Tunics

The standard tunic issued to other ranks and NCOs changed little from its introduction in 1933 until the end of World War II. Made from a coarse grey-green cloth which had a low visibility in the field, it featured an innovation for the army – an open collar which could be worn with a shirt and tie. Previously all ranks had worn an uncomfortable high-collared tunic, introduced in 1909. The new collar was of coloured felt representing the various corps and service colours. Known as the Baistrocchi pattern (after General Federico Baistrocchi, the Under Secretary of War, who headed the committee responsible for the new design), the tunic featured four pleated patch pockets and plain grey-green shoulder straps. The MVSN had the same cut, but with a plain grey-green collar. Colour cloth patches were always worn on the collar, on to which was superimposed a small silver metal five-pointed star (to signify the unity of Italy) for army personnel and a *fascio* for the Militia. The tunic was lined with linen material and had a variable number of internal pockets. The buttons were of various types – brass, green or brown plastic, or wood.

An engineer corporal major in the pre war grey/green Baistrocchi tunic. Tobruk, North Africa, 1941. (Author's collection)

The coloured collar was replaced in 1940 with a plain collar of the style already worn by the Militia. From 1940 the tunic material was made from a half-natural and half-synthetic mix. Rank chevrons were worn on both arms by NCOs. The tunic was worn on all war fronts. It was functional, though in hotter climates it was considered uncomfortable to wear.

A small metallic clothing identification tag was often sewn under the tunic collar. Written on it in indelible ink was the owner's name, unit, military district and conscription class. When a soldier was discharged from service, the tag was sewn on to the inside back cover of his individual record book for re-use in the case of future recall to arms.

Officers and warrant officers wore tailor-made tunics of similar cut to that of other ranks and NCOs, though in a lighter shade of grey-green made from a fine-weave gaberdine known as *cordellino*. These were fully lined and also had varying numbers of internal pockets.

The army Baistrocchi-pattern collar for officers was of coloured velvet with gilt stars, while MVSN officers had plain collars similar to Militia other ranks.

Detachable grey rigid cloth shoulder straps were worn. These were always piped in the corps colour, which in the case of the army matched the velvet collar. On the straps were miniatures of the headwear badge and rank insignia. Warrant officers had rank insignia only on their straps. Rank was also denoted on the forearms from the grade of officer cadet upwards. Gilt-embossed buttons were worn with this pattern tunic.

In 1940 orders from the high command for a more austere wartime pattern were introduced for combat wear. This was to be of the same material as that worn by other ranks and featured a plain non-coloured collar, plain non-rigid cloth shoulder straps, plastic buttons and smaller rank insignia on the forearms. All

Officers of a photographic section attached to the 8 Engineer Regiment wearing the officers' pattern Baistrocchi tunic. Rome, 1939. (Author's collection)

medal ribbons worn on the tunic were also reduced in size. Officers could still wear their old Baistrocchi tunic at the front line, but only if it was modified sufficiently to conform with the new wartime dress regulations.

The officers' pattern tunic was stylish, hard-wearing and generally well liked, although the close-fitting style tended to restrict freedom of movement and in warmer climates it was considered uncomfortable.

Pantaloons and Breeches

Infantry other ranks and NCOs wore ugly baggy grey-green woollen pantaloons (of the same style worn by the Italians during World War I) which reached to just below the knees. Some featured cloth loops for a leather belt, while others had buttons to secure them. All had a concealed fly front, two slash hip pockets on the side and two back pockets. The bottoms of the legs were secured by cloth ties or buttons. Although this style of leg wear had been common at the outbreak of World War II, of the main European armies only the Italians continued to use it.

Cavalry, artillery crew and some motorised troops wore more flared riding breeches, which came down lower on the leg. These had much the same fastening and pockets as the infantry pantaloons. Again these were of World War I design, although the loose style was better suited for riding horses and mounting vehicles.

Officers of the Lupi di Toscana infantry division, wearing the coarse grey/green wartime uniforms, parade with the divisional colours at Demblan, Albania, during Mussolini's visit in March 1941. (Author's collection)

The three officers on the right, atop the AB41 armoured car, are wearing the regulation breeches with stripe down the side. As they are Bersaglieri, they would have a crimson strip in the centre of the stripe. (Author's collection)

Militia other ranks and NCOs sometimes had a thin black stripe running down the outside of each leg – 2 cm wide for NCOs and 1 cm for other ranks.

A special breeches pattern was sometimes issued for use in Russia. This was grey-green on the outside, with a heavy green woollen lining. However, many soldiers went to the Russian Front wearing only the regular issue breeches, which in the sub-zero temperatures of winter proved totally inadequate.

Warrant officers and officers wore breeches made of the same grey *cordellino* as their tunics. These had a concealed fly front, usually two vertical slash hip pockets, one or two small hip fob pockets and one or two rear pockets. Although no belt was worn, buttons on the inside top made provision for elastic suspender straps. At the rear of some there was a small adjustable cloth strap. The legal bottoms had cloth ties.

All warrant officers and officers wore two black felt stripes 2 cm wide down the outside of the legs. In the

A private of the tank corps in front of a barracks entrance wears the grey/green pantaloons with puttees and black ankle boots. (Author's collection)

centre was a thin cord which matched the piping colour of the tunic. Generals had silver cord.

With the introduction of the more austere wartime pattern uniform, the wearing of stripes on *cordellino* breeches was still allowed. But the coarse woollen grey-green breeches of the same cut, also prescribed for officers, were to be worn without the stripes.

Shirts

In 1935 grey-green shirts were issued to other ranks and NCOs. Of generous length, they had an open collar and a zip front from the chest upwards, two-pleated chest patch pockets, sleeve cuffs secured by a wooden button and plain shoulder straps made from the shirt material. No insignia was worn on the shirt. A flannel version was worn in the winter and a linen one in the summer.

Another pattern introduced in 1939 was of similar design and colour but differed in having no shoulder straps and the front zip replaced by wooden buttons. A small button secured the rear of the collar to the shirt. The flannel shirt had no chest pockets.

Officers had tailor-made shirts of grey-green cotton or silk. There were many variations, however. Some had chest patch pockets, plain cloth shoulder straps and full-buttoned fronts, while others were buttoned from the waist upwards and had no shoulder straps or pockets.

An Alpini lieutenant serving on the Albanian/Greek warfront poses in a shirt displaying rank over the left pocket. 1941. (Author's collection)

When the shirt was worn without a tunic, rank insignia in the form of small embroidered stars either by themselves or contained within a rectangular box were worn horizontally over the left breast pocket region. A grey-green cummerbund could be worn with the shirt when the tunic was not worn.

One shirt peculiar to the MVSN was a black one – which in Italy signified that the wearer was a Fascist. Donned with pride by all ranks in politically based units, this symbol of the revolution was worn on all battle fronts. The shirt was adopted from the World War I Arditi, the shock troops of the Italian army, who stormed the Austrian trenches armed only with a dagger and hand grenades.

There were numerous variations, both in design and in quality. When worn, rank insignia was placed horizontally over the left breast pocket for officers, warrant officers and NCOs and was usually a smaller version of that worn on the field cap. A black cummerbund could be used with the shirt when a tunic was not worn.

Colonial Militia soldiers display a variety of uniform items unique to the CCNN. The left soldier is wearing grey/green pantaloons with a black stripe, while the man next to him has on a blackshirt. Misurata, Libya, January 1942. (Phil Wernham)

Sweaters

A number of patterns of grey knitted woollen pullover were worn. One version had a roll neck and six plastic buttons on the seam of the wearer's left shoulder. Another was an open-neck type of the same colour but without buttons. A grey-green open-neck pullover with two buttons at the front was also worn. Pullovers were on general issue to all soldiers.

A black woollen roll-neck pullover was worn by MVSN cyclists, motorcyclists and horsemen, and by Border Militia personnel. Unofficial home-knitted sweater variations were also allowed.

Greatcoats

In 1934 a greatcoat made of coarse grey-green wool was introduced for other ranks and NCOs of 'non-mounted' branches of the army. It was single-breasted, secured at the front by five plastic buttons under a concealed flap and featured a deep, open collar on which could be attached army or MVSN insignia. There were two vertical slash chest pockets and two flapped hip pockets. A flannel lining could also be attached inside for extra warmth. Shoulder straps were plain and rank insignia was worn on the upper arms. The coat's main failing was that, being single-breasted, it was not particularly warm in the colder weather.

In the same year the infantry pattern greatcoat was introduced for other ranks and NCOs of 'mounted services'. Made of the same grey-green material, it was similar in cut but featured a larger one-piece collar, bigger slit chest pockets and was more flared at the bottom.

A greatcoat for warrant officers and officers was also introduced in 1934. Made initially of a good quality light grey wool, it was double-breasted with two rows of three gilt buttons and two flapped hip pockets.

During wartime greatcoats were also made of a coarser grade grey-green wool and often had plastic or wooden buttons. On the back was an adjustable cloth belt affixed by two buttons, and below that a pleated flap which opened to the base of the coat was secured by five small buttons. These coats were warm to wear and a considerable improvement on the other ranks' pattern.

Another legacy of World War I was the coarse grey-green unlined woollen cape which came to the wearer's knees. Worn by Alpini, Bersaglieri and MVSN other ranks and NCOs, it featured a large collar on which insignia could be worn and was fastened around the throat. The cape was popular mainly with Alpini troops.

Footwear

NCOs and other ranks of all branches of the army (except Alpini) were issued leather front-lacing ankle boots, with or without hobnails on the soles. These were of the same basic construction as those used by the Italians in World War I, known as the pattern 1912. Officers could also wear this pattern of boot.

Soldiers in the infantry pattern grey/green greatcoat for other ranks and NCOs guard a railway wagon load of 1912 model 75/27 guns. (Author's collection)

Alpini of the Verona battalion, Tridentina Alpine division, dressed in the grey/green cape trudge through the cold on the Greek/Albanian front. April 1941. (Author's collection)

The boots were always dyed black if worn in Europe. A complaint from the other ranks was that the soles were sometimes made of sub-standard materials and did not stand up to the rigours of continued use.

Alpini other ranks and NCOs used pattern 1912 climbing boots of brown leather and of similar appearance to the former, though of sturdier construction and with extra hobnails for climbing. Alpini officers wore the same pattern, although they were required to buy them.

The regulation footwear for most officers was initially knee-high leather riding boots very much like those worn by German officers in World War II. These were black for European conditions. But with the introduction of the wartime uniform, high boots were often replaced with ankle boots worn with high woollen socks, and sometimes leather leggings.

The model 1929 grey-green woollen puttees, worn with ankle boots by other ranks and NCOs, wrapped from the ankle to just below the knee, where they were secured by cloth ties. Fascist Militia personnel sometimes wore black or grey-green puttees with a central black stripe. Puttees were unpopular with all who had to wear them, as it was time-consuming to put them on, and they were uncomfortable and tended to unravel – often with unfortunate results.

Black leather leggings, a hangover from the age of cavalry, were worn by officers, warrant officers, NCOs and other ranks of the Bersaglieri, infantry, cavalry, artillery, armoured and transport units. They were secured at the ankle by an internal metal clip and at the top below the knee by an external belt.

NCOs and other ranks of cavalry, armoured and motorised units wore yet another pattern of leggings known as the Model 1907. This type was secured at the base by a long leather strap which wound around the legging and buckled three-quarters of the way up. Another short belt and buckle secured the top.

Grey-green woollen knitted socks were issued to all ranks. These came in varying lengths and qualities but all had one unusual feature in common – most of the toe section was missing. There was only a small strip that fitted between the big and fourth toe. Over this area was placed a piece of cloth to absorb any sweat. It was a rather unusual idea, but one which saw widespread use. Officers bought or had made their own version of these socks.

Another style favoured by all ranks of the MVSN was a pair of long black or grey-green woollen hose over which another pair of shorter white socks was rolled down around the ankles. Black or grey-green puttees were also used in conjunction with white socks.

Sundry Items

Grey-green woollen gloves were issued to all branches of the army for wear during winter and service in cold climates. Large woollen grey-green mittens with a separate thumb and forefinger (for fitting through a rifle trigger guard) were used by soldiers on the Russian Front. These had felt inserts for extra warmth.

An unusual style of grey-green leather mittens was issued to some machine-gun or mortar crews. These had chain-mail on the bottom of the thumb, fingers and palm to give protection from burns when changing hot barrels. Paratroops adopted black leather gauntlets with woollen lining.

Officers bought their own woollen gloves, although for normal service-wear army officers and warrant officers had a brown leather pattern, while their MVSN counterparts wore black or, for service in Africa, a brown leather version.

A grey-green woollen balaclava helmet which left only the face exposed was issued to Alpini for wear in the cold, and a white woollen version also existed for snow warfare.

Tropical Uniforms

Tunics

The tropical field tunic for other ranks and NCOs was originally designed for service in the Ethiopian campaign (1935-36) and was developed with advice from the Royal Corps of Colonial Soldiers. Of a similar cut to that of the standard grey-green woollen tunic, it was made from light khaki linen. It was unlined, with a plain collar, dark brown plastic buttons and plain cloth shoulder straps. Rank insignia was worn on the upper arms by NCOs and other ranks. This basic design remained in use with some variations up to and during World War II.

The officers' tropical tunic, introduced during the Ethiopian conflict, was of much the same cut and colour as the other ranks' version of the period. It had plastic buttons, but with superior shoulder straps and rank insignia. Both these tunics were very similar in appearance to the German Afrika Korps tunic of World War II. Italian shoulder straps, however, come to a point facing the collar, whereas German ones are rounded.

During the Ethiopian campaign a tunic called a *sahariana* became popular because it was so comfort-

A medical corps second lieutenant wears the typical four-pocket tropical tunic worn by officers during the Ethiopian campaign. (Author's collection)

able to wear. Originally issued to colonial soldiers stationed in the Libyan Sahara, it was soon in widespread use throughout the army. It was a four patch pocket bush jacket with a conventional collar, although it sometimes incorporated a cloth waist belt, and had plastic buttons. A special style of breast pocket flap was used. This was a strip of material sewn over the top half of the jacket, culminating in a point over each breast pocket and continuing around the back, giving a cape-like effect.

The *sahariana* was extremely popular with officers but was also worn by all other ranks. During World War II it was used widely by the army and MVSN in North Africa, where it eventually became the official issue tunic for officers. It was even used in small numbers by the German army and Luftwaffe in North Africa. It was made from a variety of materials from light linen to burlap, and in a range of colours from olive green to sandy khaki.

An unlined pullover khaki tunic was issued to other ranks in the late 1930s; this opened to the waist and had three wooden or plastic buttons up the front, two chest and two hip patch pockets, a cloth waist belt, button-up cuffs and plain detachable cloth shoulder straps.

A dark khaki *cordellino* four-pocket tunic of the same cut as that worn by officers in Italy – though without the coloured collar – was worn in the winter by officers stationed in the colonies before World War II.

The shoulder straps worn by officers on most tropical tunics had a black cloth backing with coloured piping, branch of service badge and rank insignia. This was the standard pattern up to the rank of general.

General rank insignia worn on shoulder straps comprised a separate pattern with a silver lace strap, embroidered eagle and insignia for the different grades within that ranking.

Fascist Militia officers often wore rank insignia on the forearms as well as the shoulder straps, though in the army the normal rule was that if it was worn on the shoulder straps it was not worn on the forearms, and vice versa.

On all patterns of tropical field tunic, collar patches could be worn, though at times only the star or *fascio* was displayed.

A Bersagliere sergeant of the Trieste motorised division wears a well-worn pullover khaki tunic bleached by the sun. (Bundesarchiv, Koblenz)

Shirts

The tropical shirt for other ranks and NCOs, originally issued for the Ethiopian campaign, was made of khaki-coloured linen with an open collar, plain cloth shoulder straps, a full-buttoned front and brown plastic or wooden buttons. It came both with and without chest patch pockets. It was made of flannel for winter and linen for summer when worn in the colonies before World War II.

As with the black shirt, a black cummerbund could be utilised by Fascist Militia other ranks when a tunic was not worn.

The tropical shirt for officers had virtually the same cut as the grey-green shirt but was tailor-made of

A medical corps second lieutenant attached to the 26 battalion wears the recently introduced sahariana. In the region of Adua, Ethiopia, 1936. (Author's collection)

A divisional general wears on his tropical tunic the distinct shoulder straps for officers of general rank. (Otto Meyer)

khaki linen, wool or silk. When a tunic was not worn rank insignia was displayed over the left pocket, as with the grey-green shirt. A khaki cummerbund could also be worn.

Trousers, Breeches, Pantaloons and Shorts

The Ethiopian campaign saw the introduction of practical khaki-olive linen trousers for other ranks and NCOs. These had a concealed fly front, two vertical slash hip pockets and a rear pocket. The bottoms were worn tucked into the top of the boots. This style proved to be ideally suited for wear in the harsh African climate, affording good protection and comfort. The army reverted to pantaloons and breeches of the same style as the continental grey-green patterns, but made of light khaki linen; these were worn by other ranks and NCOs in Africa after the Ethiopian campaign.

Though there were many variations, provision was normally made for the wearing of a belt either externally or, in some cases, by threading it internally around the waist. Two vertical slash hip pockets were standard, but some styles had rear slash pockets and a small adjustable cloth belt at the rear.

The wearing of shorts by other ranks was authorised in hotter regions. These were usually from cut-down khaki pantaloons.

Tropical breeches for officers were of khaki or olive green linen for summer and *cordellino* for winter before World War II. These were of the same basic pattern as the grey *cordellino* breeches, though with no stripes.

Officers were also permitted to wear shorts in the hotter climates. These were of various materials of a khaki colour, with two slash hip pockets and two rear pockets.

An army engineer wears the typical long khaki trousers tucked into the top of high ankle boots which were worn during the Ethiopian campaign. (Author's collection)

An infantry private wearing khaki pantaloons alongside a Fiat SPA CL39 truck. (Author's collection)

Infantry soldiers holding parachute flares wear the typical desert dress for troops behind the front lines – grey/green or khaki shirts, khaki shorts, pantaloons, grey/green puttees and leather boots. Tunisia, North Africa, 1943. (Author's collection)

Footwear

Natural tan-coloured boots were worn by other ranks and NCOs during the Ethiopian campaign. These high boots came well above the ankle and laced up the front with a combination of eyelets and hooks. They proved very successful in protecting the feet and lower legs from the thorns and cacti encountered in Ethiopia.

The most common other ranks pattern ankle boot issued prior to and during World War II was the same model as that worn in Europe, but in a tan colour.

The knee-high riding boots worn by officers in the colonies were the same as the continental pattern, although in brown. However, variations were often found: some had a small lace-up section at the lower front, lacing on the upper inside edge or full lacing up the front.

Brown pull-on leather ankle boots with elastic sides were also regulation footwear available to officers in the colonies. Brown leather sandals were popular in Africa, too, primarily with native colonial soldiers, although they were also worn by Italian officers, NCOs and other ranks.

The M29 puttees were in khaki for colonial soldiers and were worn with boots, sandals or bare feet in the case of native troops.

Both patterns of leather leggings worn in Europe were issued in brown leather for Africa. A further pattern was worn by the Italian African Police. The outside was secured by leather loops which linked together and were fastened near the top by a short leather belt.

Considerable variation in items of tropical uniform was permitted in the Italian armed forces, especially during World War II, because of chronic shortages of suitable material and difficulties in shipping supplies to Africa, as many of the ships were sunk en route. This meant uniforms were often a combination of tropical and continental, whatever could be obtained. In Tunisia in 1943 many reinforcements were airlifted from Italy and arrived fully kitted out in continental uniform.

Specialised Paratroop Garments

From 1938 a khaki jump suit was worn by members of the 1 Reggimento Fanti dell'Aria in North Africa. The overalls had a zip-up chest, two zipped chest pockets and two zipped hip pockets. There were cuff straps on each arm and straps on each ankle secured by a button.

Rank insignia was worn on the arms by NCOs; officers did not wear the jump suit. The star of the Royal Army was worn on the turned-up collars after 1939, when Libyans were granted special Italian citizenship. Before that there was a small silver stylised wing worn on each collar.

A special version of the *sahariana* tunic was introduced in 1941 for wear by army paratroops in Italy. Of grey-green colour, it was of similar cut to the tropical *sahariana* worn by the army, only it had no shoulder straps or collar lapels. The tunic had two pleated chest patch pockets, two unpleated hip patch pockets and a front-fastening cloth belt. The officers' tunic was made of grey-green wool and had a concealed button flap down the front. The other ranks' version was similar but had an exposed button front.

In 1942 a khaki version of the grey-green para *sahariana* was issued for use in North Africa. This differed little in design to the grey-green version, although other ranks had exposed buttons down the front and officers sometimes a concealed button front. There was no noticeable difference in quality between other ranks' and officers' tunics apart from the insignia.

Cloth collar patches were worn on the front collar points, while rank insignia was placed on the arms in the normal manner.

New grey-green paratroop's trousers introduced in 1941 were secured by a belt around the waist and by two cords around the ankles. On the front of the trousers were two diagonal pockets, while two pockets on the rear were fastened with a button. In 1942 a khaki version was issued, incorporating a waist belt into the design.

In 1942 a camouflage jump smock for paratroops was introduced. This three-quarter-length garment was of the same material as the M1929 shelter-quarter, which had a patch pattern of forest green, chestnut brown and light grey-green. The smock buttoned up the front and had a concealed flap. A grey-green version was also made, but the patch pattern was the one most commonly used in combat and was also the first camouflage pattern garment worn by the Italian army.

Army stars were sometimes worn on the wide collars, with rank insignia for officers and NCOs on the left chest instead of the arm. The jump smock was very similar in appearance to the German paratroop jump smock.

The para jump boot was quite similar to the high ankle boot worn during the Ethiopian campaign. Worn by all ranks, it came in black leather with rubber soles and had twenty-four eyelets.

Knee pads worn during a jump were of grey cloth full of padding and with adjustable elastic bands. Although padding was also made for the elbows, shoulders and shins, only the knee pads were used to any extent.

A Libyan bugler wears the khaki jump suit of the 1 Regiment of air infantry. Castel Benito, Libya. (Bundesarchiv, Koblenz)

Protective Clothing

Armoured crew were issued a special three-quarter protective coat made of black leather. Worn by all ranks, it was double-breasted, with two rows of three black plastic buttons, an open collar, two slant hip pockets, cuff straps and a soft leather belt. Metal stars were attached to the collars and, where appropriate, a special metal version of the rank insignia for either officers or NCOs was worn. For NCOs this was on the arms, for warrant officers on the shoulder straps and for officers on the cuffs. A popular but unofficial way to wear rank insignia was on the chest.

The leather coat, though cumbersome to wear, did afford good protection inside the confines of an armoured fighting vehicle. The French army issued its tank crews with a similar style of leather coat.

Coats of the same cut, though in brown leather, were worn in Africa by motorcyclists and drivers; these were made under contract to the army by private clothing companies.

Protective one-piece overalls of grey-green or blue linen were issued to armoured crews, motorcyclists and vehicle drivers. These had two chest patch pockets, a front buttoned from the waist upwards and a cloth waist belt. They were worn for fatigue duties and in combat by armoured crews.

In 1941 a blue linen overall very similar in design to the one just described was introduced for tank personnel and units with armoured vehicles. One difference was the addition of deep pockets over each knee, with padding underneath the knees and arms for extra protection in the confined spaces of the vehicles.

The armoured car crewmen, second from the left and on the right wear the grey/green overalls common to all armoured vehicle crews. (Author's collection)

Divisional General Calvi de Bergolo (centre), commander of the Centauro armoured divison, wears the black leather three-quarter coat common to all armoured vehicle crew. Gafsa, Tunisia, February 1943. (Bundesarchiv, Koblenz)

Impermeable protective suits were supplied to special units such as chemical companies, decontamination squads and soldiers whose duties required them to remain in fixed positions. The suit consisted of an overall which extended from ankle to neck; drawstraps to close the openings; a hood which fitted tightly over the neck; gloves and boots. Made of double-woven material (Pirelli cloth) of grey-greenish colour which was rubberised on the outside and treated on the inside with a special chemical substance, these were hot and uncomfortable to wear for long periods, particularly in a harsh climate such as Libya's.

A white two-piece camouflage suit was available for snow warfare and was issued primarily to Alpini ski soldiers. Made of waterproofed material, the tunic had a hood, two chest patch pockets and a lace-up front. The trousers were straight-legged and of generous cut. Rank, when worn by officers, was either on the forearms or shown on the left breast in the form of stars.

A three-quarter-length windcheater made of a heavy-duty water-proofed hemp was introduced in 1940. It had a half buttoned-up front with plastic buttons, two chest pockets, cloth belt loops around the waist to support an equipment belt, large collars which could be closed by buttons underneath, closed cuffs, adjustable drawstrings on each side of the hip, and reinforced shoulders. Made in a range of colours from grey-green to dark grey, it was worn by officers and other ranks of the Bersaglieri, artillery personnel, engineers and MVSN combat units.

A shorter lightweight version of the windcheater was worn by Bersaglieri mounted on bicycles. It was normally used in the warmer months and differed from the foregoing in that it had a drawstring up the front instead of buttons and no belt loops, the collar was closed by a metal hook and in the sleeves was an elastic band which enabled the sleeves to be pulled up while cycling.

A three-quarter-length windcheater with an open collar was available for officers. Made of waterproofed material in a light tan or various grey-green shades, it was double-breasted with two rows of three brown plastic buttons, had two chest patch pockets and two large flapped hip patch pockets. Other versions had chest pockets and two internal slanting hip pockets or slanting hip pockets only.

A reinforcing strip of leather was sewn on each shoulder and a cloth belt worn around the waist. Rank was worn on the forearms. This tunic was popular with officers because it gave the wearer good overall protection from the elements.

Officers of the Trieste motorised division about to quench their thirst with captured beer. The man on the left wears the issued windcheater, while the other sports grey/green breeches with his tropical tunic. (Bundesarchiv, Koblenz)

Coarse grey-green woollen tunic of a sergeant of the XIII Zone (Bari) Blackshirt assault unit. The black woven rifle on the left arm indicates the wearer is a marksman.

Coarse woollen wartime tunic for a major of the tank corps. All insignia was kept to a minimum: the cuff rank is yellow cotton instead of wire wove, while the shoulder straps are plain.

A battle tunic for a Royal Army divisional general with plain shoulder straps and green plastic buttons. On the wearer's upper right arm are three oblique stripes showing the wearer was wounded three times in combat.

Above: Other ranks' grey-green wool pantaloons. This pair has a single black stripe on the outside of the legs, denoting the wearer is a member of the Fascist Militia. Right: Other ranks' grey-green wool breeches worn by soldiers of mounted formations.

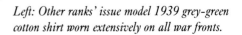

Above: Officers' grey-green breeches made of cordellino material. The yellow stripe on the side denotes the wearer is attached to the artillery. Right: Officers' breeches made of coarse grey-green wool. This was a wartime pattern and as such did not have stripes.

Left: Other ranks' issue model 1939 grey-green cotton shirt worn extensively on all war fronts.

Continental cotton shirt for officers. These shirts have much the same cut as the tropical shirts; though tailor-made the shirts conform to an officially approved pattern.

Other ranks' woollen pullover.

Black cotton shirt of the Fascist Militia. These shirts were worn by Blackshirts on all war fronts and were a symbol that embodied the Fascist revolution.

The other ranks' model 1934 infantry greatcoat was single-breasted with a concealed front. It was made of an inferior quality coarse grey-green wool.

The model 1934 greatcoat for officers was made of good quality light-coloured grey wool; it was double-breasted, the rank was worn on the forearms, and no shoulder straps were worn on the coat.

The model 1912 standard-issue leather ankle boots for other ranks. Brown were for tropical wear – in Europe the boots were black.

The model 1912 climbing boots issued to other ranks of the Alpini. Officers wore the same type but were required to purchase theirs privately.

Officers' black high boots worn with breeches.

Rear: Two types of grey-green woollen socks worn by all ranks. Front, left to right: Colonial leg wraps, grey-green for Royal Army and Militia, black for Fascist Militia.

Black leather leggings which were worn by all ranks of mounted formations.

Black leather leggings which were worn by all ranks of non-mounted and some mounted formations.

Left: Leather mitten with chain-mail. These are thought to have been issued to some mortar or machine-gun crews for handling hot barrels. Right, wool mitten with felt liner for wear in extreme cold: note finger to enable wearer to pull trigger of weapon.

Tropical tunic for a soldier of the transportation corps; the plain detachable shoulder straps are piped in blue for the transport corps.

Tropical tunic for a lieutenant of the 1 Febbraio Blackshirt division, which was raised for the Ethiopian War. This is typical of the type of tunic worn by junior officers of the Blackshirts of this period.

Tropical sahariana for a captain of the Bersaglieri; since the ranking is shown on the shoulder straps it is not displayed on the forearms.

A sahariana for a soldier of the Superga division made of burlap materials – an indication of the chronic supply shortages which faced the textile industry as the war progressed.

Pullover tunic for a soldier of the 102 Trento motorised division. This pattern of tunic was popular with soldiers. The buttons are made of wood, the shoulder straps are always plain.

Other ranks' tropical shirt. This particular shirt was picked up from a clothing dump outside El Alamein by an Australian soldier in 1942.

Officers' tropical khaki cotton shirt. These were made for the individual officer by military tailors.

Left: Typical tropical breeches worn by soldiers of mounted units. Right: Other ranks' tropical breeches with the inner legs reinforced for extra durability.

Brown leather leggings worn by mounted soldiers in the African colonies.

Officers' brown leather high boots worn in the African colonies.

Brown leather leggings worn by Italian African police personnel in the African colonies.

Model 1942 tropical paratroop sahariana without collars worn by a paratrooper of the Folgore Division in North Africa.

Brown leather jacket of the exact same cut as the black tank jacket. This jacket was worn by motorcyclists in Africa.

The black leather tank jacket was worn by all armoured vehicle crews. This tunic is for a second lieutenant, as denoted by the special metal version of the rank bar on the forearms.

PLATE I

HANDBOOK ON THE ITALIAN MILITARY FORCES

ARMY SERVICE DRESS AND FIELD UNIFORMS

Commissioned Officers

INSIGNIA ON HEADGEAR
General officer

COLLAR PATCH
1st Cavalry

BRIGADIER GENERAL

LIEUTENANT COLONEL, CAVALRY

INSIGNIA OF RANK

SERVICE CAP BAND
Brigadier general

SLEEVE INSIGNIA
Brigadier general

SECOND LIEUTENANT, INFANTRY

INSIGNIA OF RANK

INSIGNIA ON GARRISON CAP
Captain

INSIGNIA ON
ALPINE TYPE OF CAP

Colour plate from the American Joint Army Navy intelligence book on the Italian Army. Top left figure is wearing service dress of a Royal Army general; lower centre figure is an officer with a greatcoat and steel helmet; top right figure is wearing uniform without tunic, rank insignia is displayed on shirt.

Top left figure is a Bersagliere wearing the Baistrocchi tunic; the lower centre figure is wearing grey-green dress without tunic; top right figure, an Alpini wearing the post-1940 style uniform.

PLATE II

ARMY FIELD UNIFORMS

Noncommissioned Officers and Enlisted Men

INSIGNIA OF RANK

SHOULDER STRAP
Marshals
(Ordinary marshal)

CHEVRONS
Noncommissioned officers
(Sergeant)

BERSAGLIERI
Marshal, old-style coat

ALPINI
Sergeant-major, new-style coat

HEADGEAR

FEZ OF BERSAGLIERI

HAT OF BERSAGLIERI

SUMMER UNIFORM
Private, Infantry

HEADGEAR

CAP OF FRONTIER GUARDS

HAT OF CARABINIERI

PLATE IV

MISCELLANEOUS ARMY AND BLACK SHIRT UNIFORMS

CRASH HELMET
Tank troops

GAS MASK
With canister

COLLAR PATCH
Tank troops

COLLAR PATCH
Chemical troops

UNIFORM OF TANK CREWS
Private, leather coat

PROTECTIVE SUIT
Private, chemical troops

BLACK SHIRT INSIGNIA

BLACK SHIRT COLLAR PATCH

SERVICE CAP BAND
Brigadier general

SLEEVE INSIGNIA
Brigadier general

FASCIST MILITIA
Private

BLACK SHIRT INSIGNIA

INSIGNIA ON GARRISON CAP
Captain

SHOULDER STRAP
Marshal major

SLEEVE INSIGNIA
Lance-corporal

Top left figure is wearing the typical uniform of an armoured crewman; lower centre figure is wearing combat uniform of a Blackshirt. Top right figure is wearing a protective suit of the chemical corps.

Artillery officer wearing the tropical sahariana, Sam Browne belt and other ranks pattern pith helmet.

A model 1933 steel helmet which has unofficially attached a metal badge for a NCO of the 2 Legion of the colonial militia which was stationed in Misurata, Libya.

Sand-painted model 1933 steel helmet for the 46 Regiment of artillery attached to the Trento motorised division which fought in North Africa during World War II. The helmet lugs are of a non-standard pattern.

A model 1941 paratroop helmet with rolled leather nose protection pad on the front and improved leather Y straps which gave better support for the wearer.

A model 1933 steel helmet for a Bersagliere of the 5 Regiment attached to the Centauro armoured division. The attached traditional cockerel plume is much in evidence.

The black leather crash helmet for armoured vehicle crews. This rather archaic though functional helmet was worn extensively by most crew members of armoured fighting vehicles.

The black leather crash helmet worn by motorcyclists. A brown leather version was issued for service in Africa.

Grey peaked cap for a major of the paratroops. Note the high sweeping crown of the cap, giving it a more Germanic appearance.

Peaked cap of a Royal Army brigade general. The silver woven lace band, called greca, was traditional for generals. The thin cords around the top of the greca denoted the grade. Brigade general had one; divisional general two; army corps general three; while a Marshal of Italy had four.

A peaked cap of an NCO of the Fascist Militia with silver badge and matching buttons. The plain band denoting the ranking is clearly visible.

Peaked cap of a captain of the Railway Militia. The flat-topped cap was more in keeping with the earlier style of cap before the German influence was introduced.

Model 1934 grey-green wool bustina for other ranks, this one being for the Chemical Corps.

High-quality continental bustina for a captain of the 10 Cavalry Regiment Vittorio Emanuele II.

Khaki peaked cap of a lieutenant of the Colonial Infantry; the cap was mainly worn out of the line as the bustina had replaced the cap on active service during World War II. The embroidered badge is for soldiers of the Royal Corps of Colonial Troops. The centre disc is red for Italian personnel, Libyan soldiers and headquarters staff.

Khaki peaked cap with brown visor for a lieutenant-colonel of the Tank Corp. The cross indicated the wearer was not assigned to a specific regiment or was in an administrative position or attached to a school.

Left: Tropical bustina for a brigade general. The ranking and eagle of this particular cap, attached by domes, could be removed when the cap was washed. Right: Continental bustina of an army general; the eagle is in gold with red backing, denoting the wearer's superior rank.

Tropical bustina for a Blackshirt; the material is light cotton while the badge is brass instead of black rayon. Right: Winter-weight tropical bustina made of khaki wool for a lieutenant of the 2 Cavalry Regiment Piemonte Reale.

Model 1942 tropical bustina with stiff visor for a second lieutenant of an unassigned divisional artillery unit. The rank stars are in metal instead of the more normal embroidered type Right: Another model 1942 bustina; this one is for a Royal Army brigade general.

A model 1942 tropical bustina of a colonel in command of the 63 Colonial Infantry Regiment. This pattern has a soft visor similar to the cap worn by the German Afrika Korps.

Other ranks pattern pith helmet for an engineer. The stencil is less common than the metal badge which is normally worn.

Standard pattern pith helmet for other ranks, this one being for a Bersagliere of the 7 Regiment attached to the Trento motorised division.

Officers were allowed to purchase their own pith helmets privately; many of them were imported from India, as was this one for an officer of the 3 Legion of the Colonial Militia stationed in Benghazi, Libya.

The Aden-pattern pith helmet for a Royal Army general. A stamped brass badge was sometimes worn instead of an embroidered one.

NCO's Alpini-style cap for a member of the Border Militia, 8 Legion Cacciatori delle Alpi. The black piping was used only by the Fascist Militia.

Left: Black felt fez with black wool tassel for other ranks and NCOs of the Blackshirt battalions and members of the regiment Giovani Fascisti. Right: Red felt fez for other ranks and NCOs of the Bersaglieri.

Left: OTO model 1935 grenade; centre: SRCM model 1935; right: Breda model 1935. These grenades relied mainly on blast, which was fair, with a good deal of smoke and noise.

The Breda Model 30 was the primary light machine gun used by the Italian Army during World War II, although it suffered from a bad reputation for reliability due to ammunition stoppages in the firing mechanism it was used on all war fronts.

Model 1937 Breda 8 mm medium machine-gun. The tripod-mounted, gas-operated, air-cooled medium machine-gun had a theoretical maximum rate of fire of 450 rounds per minute. The model 1937 had a reputation for being reliable and was one of the best machine-guns the Italian armed forces possessed.

Top: Model 91/41 Carcano 6.5 mm calibre service rifle. Centre: Model 91/38 Carcano carbine 7.35 mm calibre with permanently attached folding spike bayonet. Bottom: Model 1891 Carcano carbine 6.5 mm calibre with spike bayonet.

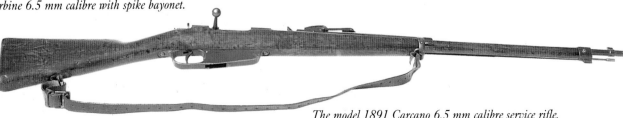

The model 1891 Carcano 6.5 mm calibre service rifle.

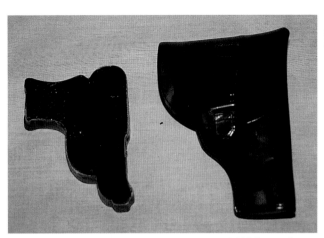

Cast fake pistol in the outline of a Beretta Model 1934 worn by an Italian officer as a non-regulation lightweight alternative to the original when on duty around the barracks.

The Model 1910 automatic pistol with its seven shot butt magazine and leather holster. Although fairly popular this pistol was not widely used by front line soldiers during World War II.

The Model 1889 Glisenti revolver was an old fashioned revolver which was still being used by the Italian armed forces in limited numbers during World War II. The revolver photographed is a variation known as the Light Type 1889 which had a slightly shorter barrel than the conventional Glisenti but retained all the basic features of this revolver.

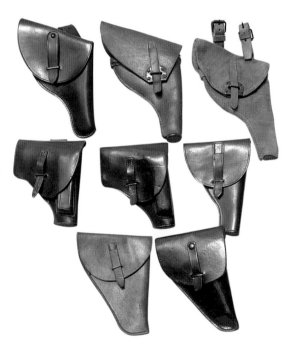

The Model 1934 Beretta automatic pistol was the most popular side arm used by the Italian armed forces. The pistol illustrated has Royal Army markings and was manufactured in 1942.

Top row: left, brown leather Glisenti model 1889 revolver holster, green leather Glisenti revolver holster, webbing Glisenti revolver holster for attaching to model 1891 bandolier. Middle row: left, grey-green leather model 1934 Beretta automatic pistol holster, brown leather Beretta pistol holster, brown leather Beretta pistol holster without external pouch for ammunition magazine clip. Bottom row: left, variation of Beretta holster without pouch; right, black leather Beretta holster used by Carabinieri and Fascist Militia.

Left to right: Carcano model 1891 leather bayonet scabbard with green leather frog; Carcano M91 fluted steel scabbard with brown leather frog for colonial use; M91 Carcano bayonet which could be used with either of the former scabbards; blued metal scabbard with belt loop for model 1938 Carcano bayonet; Carcano M38 bayonet with folding blade; scabbard and M38 bayonet with non-folding blade.

Left to right: Scabbard and model 1925 dagger first issued for wear by officers of the Colonial Blackshirt Militia (this pattern was also later worn by Libyan Colonial paratroops); scabbard and model 1935 dagger worn by other ranks of the Fascist Militia; scabbard and model 1939 dagger widely issued to Blackshirts, Royal Army assault soldiers and army paratroops.

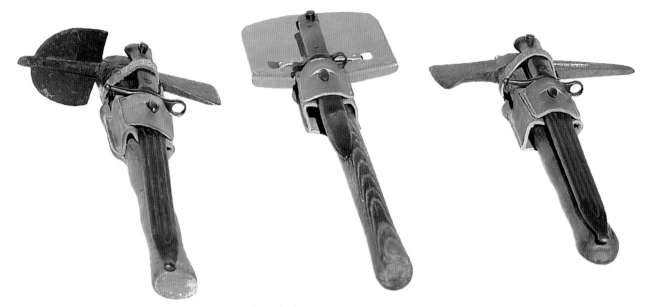

Three types of entrenching tool with a combination frog which could also carry a bayonet.

Model 1891 two-pocket bandolier.

Model 1874/89 three-pocket grey-green leather cavalry bandolier. A pistol holster could be attached to the terminal ring at the bottom.

Model 1891 brown leather two-pocket cavalry bandolier for colonial use.

Unofficial pattern of bandolier worn by Fascist Militia.

Model 1891 grey-green leather belt with model 1907 cartridge pouches. This was the standard rig issued to all infantry.

White canvas cartridge pouch and belt worn by Alpini ski soldiers.

Left: Canvas and leather pouch for carrying the magazine clips for the model 1938 MAB; a leather neck strap could be connected with the D ring when worn with another pouch. Right: leather tool pouch for Breda model 1930 6.5 mm light machine-gun.

The model 1939 rucksack was a large-capacity pack with two side pockets. Though primarily issued to Alpini it was also used by other soldiers. This particular pack was picked up in North Africa by a New Zealand soldier.

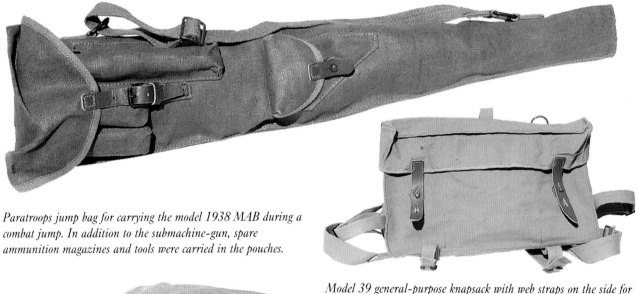

Paratroops jump bag for carrying the model 1938 MAB during a combat jump. In addition to the submachine-gun, spare ammunition magazines and tools were carried in the pouches.

Model 39 general-purpose knapsack with web straps on the side for attaching a rolled greatcoat, camouflage shelter-quarter or blanket.

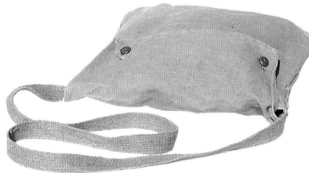

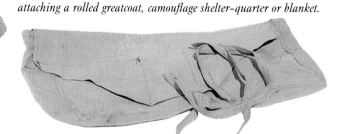

Cotton drill tactical bag used by soldiers to carry ammunition and food in the front line.

This canvas pouch was used to carry items of spare or dirty clothing in the pack.

Model 1933 gas-mask was contained in a canvas bag which divided into two segments, one to house the mask piece, the other the filter cylinder with a length of corrugated rubber hosing which connected to the mask when in use.

The type 35 gas-mask was contained in the single-compartment canvas bag; the mask piece and filter cylinder screwed directly into each other.

Large-capacity 6½-litre aluminium water containers of this type were used in North Africa.

Left to right: Water bottle with strap attached to wool cover (this is a conversion of the bottle illustrated far right); large-capacity water bottle used by Alpini; most commonly encountered water bottle used by Italian army; water bottle used in Ethiopia.

Green-painted two-piece mess tin with aluminium drinking cup.

Personnel equipment: small fold-out dish warmer, which was heated by solid fuel cubes; Royal Army-marked aluminium fork and spoon set.

Continental model 1929 camouflage shelter-quarter used in Europe and Africa.

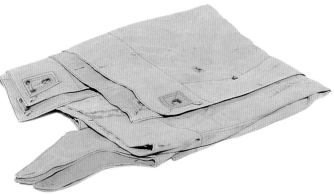

Tropical tan version of the shelter-quarter issued for use in Africa.

Personal issue items; woollen blanket; tent-pole sections – three per soldier to use with camouflage shelter-quarter; field dressings – at least one per man.

Left: 8 × 30 prismatic binoculars of the standard patterns used by officers; Right: Royal Army-marked compass.

Two patterns of leather map case which could be purchased by officers.

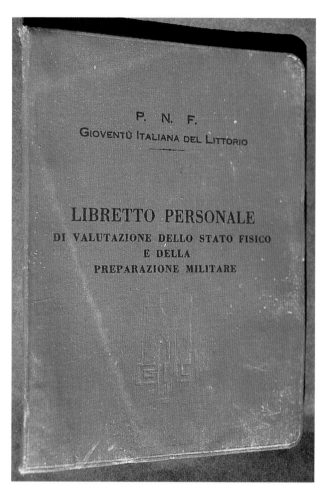

Other ranks' individual record book.

Fascist Youth evaluation record book for all male citizens aged eleven to thirty-two.

Letters sent to soldiers serving in North Africa.

MVSN ID book.

Inset of MVSN ID book.

Pay book for warrant officers and officers, is.

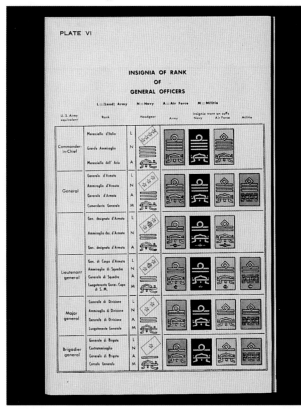

Colour plates from American Joint Army Navy intelligence book on the Italian Army, illustrating the insignia of other ranks, NCOs and warrant officers.

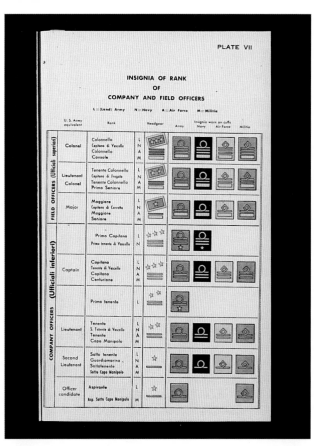

A chart of the rank insignia of officers.

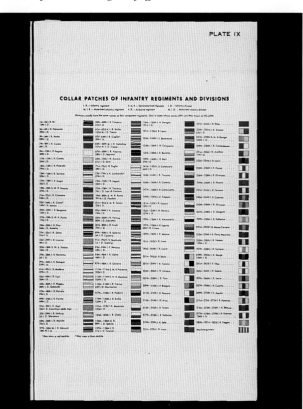

Comparable chart showing rank insignia of generals.

Plates displaying the collar patches of regiments and divisions.

Standard-issue dog tag for Italian soldiers during World War II. This was worn around the neck at all times and carried the wearer's military serial number, code number of military district, religion, full name, parents' names, year of birth, home town and province. The disc could be split into two identical plates, one of which would be kept with the body and the other sent home with the deceased's personal effects.

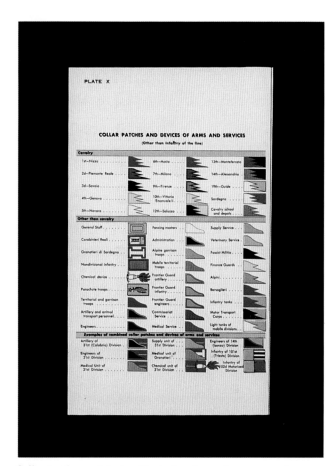

Collar patches and devices illustrating the various arms and services.

Top left: Woven synthetic thread shield of a soldier of the Marmarica Division, one of four metropolitan infantry divisions stationed in Libya.
Top right: Stamped brass shield for a soldier of the Trento motorised division stationed in Libya.
Bottom left: Gold wire-embroidered felt cloth shield of an officer of the Sirte Division, another of the metropolitan infantry divisions stationed in Libya.
Bottom right: Stamped brass shield for other ranks of the Celere Duca Principe Amedeo D'Aosta Division, one of the three Celere divisions.

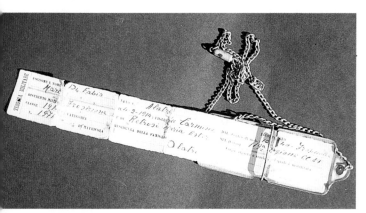

Locket-type dog tag worn during World War I and II; it contained much the same information as the stamped metal type with the addition of the name of the unit to which the soldier was initially assigned.

Below, right:
Top left: A silver wire-embroidered felt cloth shield for officers of 1 Febbraio Blackshirt division which served in the Ethiopian campaign.
Top right: A stamped brass shield for an assault soldier of the 10 Blackshirt Zone, whose headquarters were in Rome.
Bottom left: Stamped aluminium arm shield for a member of the Anti-Aircraft Militia.
Bottom right: Stamped aluminium arm shield for the CCNN 21 Aprile Libica Blackshirt division which served in Libya.

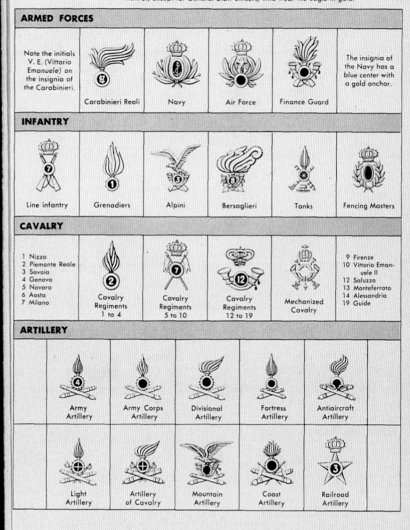

Plates from the American Joint Army Navy intelligence book on the Italian Army. A selection of headwear badges is shown.
While the variety illustrated is not exhaustive, it does show basic pattern types worn by all ranks of many of the arms and services.

PLATE XII

INSIGNIA OF ARM OR SERVICE

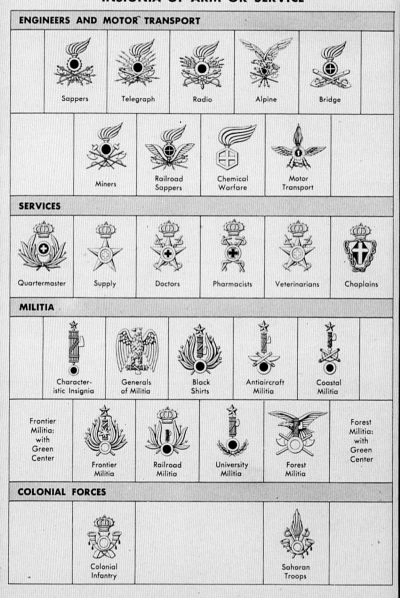

ENGINEERS AND MOTOR TRANSPORT

Sappers · Telegraph · Radio · Alpine · Bridge

Miners · Railroad Sappers · Chemical Warfare · Motor Transport

SERVICES

Quartermaster · Supply · Doctors · Pharmacists · Veterinarians · Chaplains

MILITIA

Characteristic Insignia · Generals of Militia · Black Shirts · Antiaircraft Militia · Coastal Militia

Frontier Militia: with Green Center · Frontier Militia · Railroad Militia · University Militia · Forest Militia · Forest Militia: with Green Center

COLONIAL FORCES

Colonial Infantry · Saharan Troops

Chapter Four
Headwear

Steel Helmets

THE COUNTRY'S first modern Italian steel helmet, known as the model 1916, was a copy of the French World War I Adrian pattern which the Italians used before manufacturing their own version. It comprised a one-piece stamped shell with a crimped rim and a separate comb welded to the dome.

The liner was either light brown leather or a hard canvas tarpaulin material with corrugated bands. The grey-green leather chinstrap had a steel fastener rather than a buckle.

An anti-aircraft battery crew, wearing the M33 steel helmet, search the skies for hostile aircraft on a small island in the Mediterranean. 7 August, 1943. (Authors' collection)

The Alpini affixed to the left side of the helmet their traditional feather, while the plumes of the Bersaglieri were attached on the right side by a variety of supporting devices.

The helmets were grey-green for army field wear and black for the Fascist Militia. Between 1921 and 1925 regulations allowed the use of brass- or silver-stamped badges and insignia on the front for each branch of the service. Also authorised was a black painted stencil for the army and a yellow version for the militia.

The helmet was widely worn during the Spanish Civil War and during World War II by anti-aircraft and army Medical Corps personnel.

In 1933 a new helmet was introduced. This modern-looking version had a deep one-piece stamped nickel steel shell with an uncrimped rim, which afforded good overall protection to the wearer. Three rivets which doubled as air vents secured the metal liner band to the helmet. The liner was leather with eight full tongues, perforated and tightened with a leather or fabric drawstring.

The chinstrap was grey-green leather for the army and black leather for the MVSN, both with the same pattern steel chinstrap buckle. (The helmet design was so successful that the same design is still in use today in the Italian armed forces.)

The army helmet was grey-green for field wear and black for the Fascist Militia until 1939, when the MVSN version was repainted to bring it in line with that of the army. A stencil was usually painted on the front. Stamped metal badges were also used – though these were unofficial. In North Africa helmets were sometimes a sandy yellowish colour. On the Russian Front they were painted white during the winter months.

Four-piece cloth helmet covers were issued to the Alpini who used white covers for snow warfare.

In 1942 a helmet cover made of M29 camo quarter-shelter material was issued for use on the M33 helmet. This had two vertical cloth loops for attaching foliage.

The Alpini utilised two types of feather holders, both affixed to the helmet, on which to secure the feather they traditionally wore. The first was a simple sheet-metal bracket with a tunnel-like section into which the feather slid. This was welded to the left side of the helmet. The other was a special arsenal feather holder secured from both the exterior and interior of the shell with a hinge section.

The Bersaglieri had a special plume holder affixed to the helmet, inside and out, on the right side. However, some plumes were simply attached directly into the air vent and secured with a wire on to the liner. Although a set of feathers was issued officially,

Two Bersaglieri wear grey/green painted M33 steel helmets with black painted stencils on the front and cockerel plumes on the side. (Bundesarchiv, Koblenz)

A member of the 285 Folgore paratroop battalion wears the M38 paratrooper helmet. 5 March, 1943. Tunisia. (Bundesarchiv, Koblenz)

soldiers could buy their own privately if they wished – officers usually wore quite opulent plumes. The Bersaglieri tradition of wearing the plume began in 1836. They were intended originally as camouflage designed to blend in with the vegetation, the idea being that hidden soldiers could spring out of the under-growth and surprise the enemy.

A paratroop helmet was introduced in 1938 for airborne soldiers; it was a one-piece stamped steel shell following the general outline of the M33 helmet, though not as deep and with the rim cut flat all round. The liner was leather, with a circular rubber-padded interior under the dome. Eight rubber pad strips evenly spaced around the rim began from the liner circle and were covered with leather for approximately 75 mm before tapering into the rubber dome circle. The grey-green leather chinstraps were a 'Y' arrange-ment which buckled on the wearer's left. This strap was riveted to the vent plugs. A fibre canopy neck-flap was attached to the back of the straps. The helmet was

painted grey-green for army paratroops. A stencil was issued by the Carabinieri only – their corps badge of a black flaming bomb.

A further version introduced in 1941 was almost the same as the M38 except for the following details; a thick rolled grey-green leather pad similar in appear-ance to a sausage filled with rubber or horsehair attached to the front just under the rim to protect the wearer's nose during landing; a slightly different arrangement of 'Y' straps which criss-crossed over the neck, giving better support, and the fibre neck-flap dispensed with. The general appearance of the para helmet was similar to its German equivalent, though not so flared around the rim.

A cloth camouflage cover was issued in late 1942. This was of the same cloth as that used on the M29 camo quarter shelter, with two horizontal straps sewn around the cover on to which foliage could be attached.

Crash Helmets

Armoured vehicle crews were issued with a deep-domed fibre crash helmet covered with black leather. A thick padded rim ran around the crown, and on the rear was a leather neck-flap which extended backwards from the ears. Above the crown padding on each side was a metal, gauze-covered air-hole.

The liner was of leather with an adjustable cord, while a leather strap with integral ear-flaps and a buckle on the left secured the helmet around the chin. This rather old-fashioned crash helmet was worn extensively by armoured vehicle crews long after similar helmets worn by contemporary armies had been discarded. It did offer good protection to the head and neck of the wearer. Bersaglieri attached to armoured formations wore the traditional cockerel feather plume on the side.

A similar helmet to that of the armoured vehicle crew was worn by motorcyclists. This had many of the same basic features, although a soft leather visor was worn on the front and the leather neck-flap was replaced with a smaller elasticised leather type forming part of the ear-flaps, which were in turn attached to the chinstraps.

A leather loop was sewn to the front of the dome, on to which a brass headwear badge could be attached. Black and brown leather versions were made, the brown version specifically for tropical service.

Continental Peaked Caps

A peaked service cap for warrant officers and officers was introduced in 1933 to replace the képi. Early patterns had low crowns, giving the cap an almost flat-topped look. Later the crown became higher and the shape took on a distinctly Germanic appearance which reflected the influence of Germany on its Axis partner. Both types were worn throughout the Fascist era. During World War II, the peaked cap was only worn out of the front line.

Paratroops of the Folgore parachute division man an anti-tank emplacement. Two wear the M42 cloth camouflage cover over their helmets. North Africa, 1942. (Bundesarchiv, Koblenz)

Marshal Emilo De Bono and the Governor of Libya, Marshal Italo Balbo, inspect troops at the Moccagatta Barracks, Tripoli. The distinctive tanker crash helmet is clearly in evidence being worn by the tank crews in the foreground. (Achille Rastelli)

The grey-green cap had a black leather peak and a chinstrap secured on the sides by a small gold button embossed with the wearer's headwear badge. The corp headwear badge on the front was made of embroidered gold wire.

A gold rank braid around the base, a combination of wide and narrow bands, was worn by warrant officers and officers up to the rank of general. For combat personnel the line dividing the band was the same colour as the cap. For service corps it was that of the corp piping – red for medical, light blue for veterinary, dark blue for supply and administration, violet for commissariat. A colonel commanding a regiment or similar unit wore red lines.

Royal Army generals' peaked caps were similar to those of lower-ranked officers, except that a silver lace band around the cap base replaced the gold rank bands. Known as *greca*, this ornament evolved from the embroidery worn by generals in the Sardinian army of the nineteenth century.

Army generals wore a badge of a special pattern unique to their rank on all their headwear. Only the

A brigade general wears the distinctive visor cap for generals. (Author's collection)

badge varied. The design was an eagle with out-stretched wings with the Cross of Savoy on its chest. The eagle's head faced the wearer's right and was surmounted by the royal crown. For brigade and divisional generals it was embroidered in silver wire on red felt backing (red indicated a command rank), gold wire on red for generals of army corps up to Marshals of Italy. General staff officers had the same style eagle in gold, but on a grey-green felt backing.

Although members of the Port, Road and Railway Militia had worn a peaked cap since 1931 it was not until 1938 that the Fascist Militia adopted one for normal service wear, where applicable, for all soldiers from NCO rank upwards.

For NCOs a single thin black cord ran around the top and bottom of the grey-green cap band, with the headwear badge in silver. A black leather chinstrap was secured by silver buttons. Adjutants wore a single silver

and black variegated stripe, a silver headwear badge and silver buttons.

Officers had gold headwear badges and buttons, while black piping ran around the crown of the cap for all those up to the rank of general. The rank bands were gold like those of the Royal Army, except that black lines rather than grey-green ones separated the bands. In 1940 the black piping around the crown was abolished.

Fascist Militia generals, like their army counterparts, had distinctive patterns of insignia for their rank. An eagle was embroidered in gold wire, the eagle's wings folded downwards, the head faced to the wearer's right while the talons clutched a *fascio*. The badge was backed by red felt. The cap featured gold piping around the crown and a black cap band with gold piping top and bottom. The chin cords were two interwoven double cords for a Luogotente Generale, double gold cords for a Console Generale and black leather for the rest. All had gold buttons.

In 1940 – in line with the rest of the MVSN – the gold piping around the cap crown was removed. All chinstraps were now of black leather and a different type of ranking called *greca littoria* was introduced. This was embroidered in gold and consisted of a series of lozenges which ran around the band. Inside each lozenge was a vertically sitting *fascio*. Above the *greca* ran thin gold cords, the number depending on the rank. The eagle remained unchanged.

Continental Side Caps

A side cap called a *bustina* was introduced in 1934 for field wear for all ranks. This replaced the peaked cap for officers in the field. It had a rounded front visor-flap of one- or two-piece construction which could be pulled down as a peak. Over the crown was an ear- and neck-flat which fastened under the chin by a button or domes. (This concept was used on the British side cap as well.) A leather sweat-band ran around the inside rim of the cap, which was lined with either cotton or silk.

For other ranks and NCOs the side cap was made of coarse grey-green wool. On the front was sewn a black rayon headwear badge for other ranks, a yellow embroidered thread badge for army NCOs and a silver one for their Militia counterparts. Up to 1938 MVSN NCOs wore rank insignia on the left side, while those in the army wore none on these caps.

The officers' pattern *bustina* was initially made of

Benito Mussolini, wearing the bustina of a Marshal of the Empire, visits the Lupi di Toscana division stationed on the Greek-Albanian front in March 1941. (Author's collection)

good quality grey cloth for ranks from warrant officer to Marshal of the Empire. This was changed to a coarse grey-green material during World War II, but came in a variety of styles and patterns.

Militia adjutants and army warrant officers wore gold badges the same as those of officers up to the rank of general.

Rank insignia was worn on the left in both the army and the militia, although in 1938 the MVSN's separate ranking system was amended in line with that of the army.

In the 1930s a black *bustina* became popular and was worn with the field uniform by officers of the MVSN and the CCNN battalions.

The wool-lined version worn in Russia had coarse grey-green wool material on the outside, although like other items of cold-weather clothing it was often a case of too little too late.

In 1942 a *bustina* with a permanently stiffened cloth visor was introduced. This was fundamentally the same as the earlier version, but it had an adjustable cloth chin-cord over the front of the visor. It was worn by both army and militia officers.

During World War II the gold and silver wire embroidery was replaced with black, yellow or white rayon badges in line with the wartime uniform regulations.

The standard pattern grey-green and khaki *bustina* were worn by Italian volunteers during the Spanish Civil War and featured Spanish Phalangist ranking on the front.

The *bustina* design was simple and practical and continued to be worn until the end of World War II.

Tropical Peaked Caps

The tropical version of the officers' peaked cap was the same as the grey-green continental version, except for the cloth colouring, which varied from olive green to sandy khaki. The visor and chinstrap were normally brown leather, although black was sometimes used. The ranking was exactly the same for the army and militia, but the stripes between the rank bands were khaki in colour.

Army generals wore a peaked cap in khaki which was similar to their continental version except for the khaki cloth and brown leather visor and chinstrap.

In 1938 a peaked cap in khaki with gold *greca littoria* was introduced for CCNN generals stationed in Africa. The cap eagle was similar to the continental

pattern with addition of the royal crown, which was bestowed in recognition of the services performed by the militia in the Ethiopian campaign.

Tropical Side Caps

Bustina manufactured for tropical wear were exactly the same as the grey-green continental versions. The majority were made from lightweight khaki cotton twill of varying quality, but during World War II some were made of burlap.

The *bustina* normally had a leather or cloth sweat-band. A variety of coloured linings was used – from khaki and olive green to red, which was found to be the best colour for the African climate as it helped keep the wearer cool while assisting the loss of heat through the top of the head.

Two brothers serving with the 80 artillery regiment, La Spezia division, wear the tropical M1929 airforce pattern Bustina. (Author's collection)

A variation for other ranks and officers was issued in 1929. This had no front visor, ear- or neck-flap; instead it had an open side or sewn panel all round the cap. This style of *bustina* was worn by the Royal Italian Air Force, although it was smaller than the army pattern.

Officers could wear a khaki wool sidecap in the cooler African months which was exactly the same cut as the cotton twill pattern. A khaki version of the grey-green M42 *bustina* with stiff cloth visor was also manufactured for officers.

Another version introduced in 1942 was similar in style to the 1934 *bustina*, but in khaki cloth with a soft permanent visor, ear-flaps and a fold-down cover for the back of the neck. This cap was similar in outline to the cap worn by the German Afrika Korps.

A Fiat Spa 38R truck carries a group of Italian POWs. The front two are wearing the M42 soft-visored tropical bustina. Tunisia, North Africa, 20 May, 1943. (ATL, Wellington, New Zealand)

Tropical rank insignia and headwear badges were manufactured in the same way as the continental patterns, the only difference being the cloth backing, which was normally khaki. Grey-green-backed badges were worn when the khaki ones were unavailable. Metal badges were also worn on the *bustina*, especially by the MVSN soldiers.

Both peaked and side caps were manufactured locally in centres such as Asmara in Ethiopia and Benghazi in Libya by tailors such as Unione Militare; they were however very reliant on Italy for all their raw materials, which had to be imported.

Pith Helmets

The pith helmet was an integral part of the Italian colonial uniform. Rather archaic in design, it continued to be worn as a light, practical form of shelter from the harsh sun, although the protection it gave from shrapnel was minimal and during World War II its use in combat was finally discontinued.

The standard pattern worn by other ranks and NCOs, known as the model 1935, was khaki cotton twill over cork. It was deep in the skull and had a wide neck and a brim which came around to form a point in the front. Other features included a khaki-painted metal ventilation knob on the top; a mesh-covered eyelet halfway down each side; a single cloth band around the base; a small square cloth pouch centre bottom on the wearer's right for holding the plumage of the *Bersaglieri* or the *nappine* and feather of the Alpini. An adjustable leather chinstrap was usually left hooked over the front rim and there was green cloth on the underside of the helmet, together with a leather sweat-band.

The headwear badge worn on the front of the helmet was of stamped brass or black rayon cotton, and was often superimposed over a cotton rosette with the Italian national colours of red, white and green. The Fascist Militia did not always wear a rosette, but when they did it was sometimes entirely of black.

Some pith helmets had a black stencil applied to the front, much like that used on steel helmets, although this was not as widespread as the use of metal badges. Soldiers also unofficially drew their own ink stencils of their particular headwear badge on the helmet. Others wrote the names and dates of battles they had participated in or – though this was frowned upon by the High Command – attached souvenir enemy badges to the sides. The wearing of these badges on a belt was

more common. Some pinned a simple holy medal on the side, perhaps hoping for a form of protection the helmet did not provide.

A private of divisional artillery with an unofficial hand-drawn stencil badge on his pith helmet. North Africa. (Otto Meyer)

One widely worn regulation pith helmet for officers was known as the Aden pattern. Many variations to the basic design can be found, but generally it was of khaki cloth-covered cork, with a flatter crown than the other ranks' pattern. On some versions cotton stitching criss-crossed the whole helmet, giving a diamond-chequered effect.

There was a cloth-covered ventilation knob at the top, a layered cloth band around the base and sometimes a purely decorative leather strap which ran from left to right over the helmet through the ventilation knob. Two small eyelets were located on either side of the strap. There was an adjustable brown leather chinstrap, again normally hooked over the front rim. On the underside of the rim was green cloth with a leather sweat-band and a silk lining in white.

Officers were, however, allowed considerable freedom in choice of the pith helmet they wore. Many bought civilian models in Italy or versions imported from India (Bombay in particular) before World War

A Bersagliere motorcyclist sports the tropical pith helmet with cockerel plumes and goggles. Egypt, North Africa. (Bundesarchiv, Koblenz)

Officers serving in East Africa often wore a variety of headwear, as this photograph in Ethiopia in January 1938 illustrates. (Author's collection)

II. Officers en route to East Africa often bought them in Port Said – these had also been imported from India. Some just wore the Truppa pattern with officer-quality insignia.

The headwear badge on the front of the helmet was the type worn on the peaked cap, usually backed with khaki cloth, although grey-green-backed badges and brass Truppa-pattern versions were also used.

Generals wore their distinctive style of eagle on the pith helmet without a rosette. Those in the army had a stamped brass or embroidered version, while the MVSN generals had an embroidered badge only.

Alpine Caps

The traditional headwear worn by the Alpini – a grey-green felt cap with the rim turned up at the back – was considered by mountain soldiers the most important part of their uniform.

The pattern worn by other ranks had a grey-green leather strap around the crown. On the front was a black rayon headwear badge and on the left an oval woollen *nappine,* the colour of which indicated a speciality – engineers, chemical service, artillery or Alpini battalion.

The officer cap was much the same style, though of a lighter shade and better quality material and with a gold-embroidered headwear badge. The rim was trimmed with grey silk ribbon, as was the crown. A small plaited grey silk cord was attached to the front base of the crown. A brass *nappine* embossed with the Cross of Savoy was worn on the left with a feather. Generals wore a silver *nappine* embossed with the cross.

A feather was traditionally worn in the *nappine*: a crow feather by other ranks and NCOs, an eagle feather by officers and a goose feather by generals.

Members of the 3 Legion, Anti-Aircraft Militia wear the MVSN pattern Alpini-style cap. Italy. (Author's collection)

Alpini who attended a rock-climbing course had their cap feather cut in a special way to indicate successful completion.

Rank badges for warrant officers and officers worn on the Alpini cap comprised a variable number of gold chevrons shaped like an inverted 'V'. These were worn on the wearer's left. Generals wore a silver lace-weave rhomboidal box with the appropriate number of stars inside indicating their rank.

The Alpine-style cap was much prized and worn by other branches of the army, especially the Frontier and Finance Guards. Various Fascist Militias used it, including the railway, road, post and telegraph, forestry, border, university and anti-aircraft units. The Militia cap was made of grey-green felt of varying quality depending on rank, and the rim was trimmed with black silk ribbon, as was the crown. A small plaited black silk cord was attached to the front base of the crown.

Rank insignia used on the cap by the Fascist Militia was similar in appearance to the army ranking chevron pattern.

An Alpini lieutenant wearing the traditional headwear of the Alpine soldier looks out from his dugout on the Greek-Albanian front January 1941. (Author's collection)

Fez

The fez was an item of headwear peculiar to some units of the army and the Fascist Militia. The Bersaglieri wore a fez of soft red felt with a long blue woollen tassel. This was originally worn in the Crimean War and was adopted from the French Zouave (colonial infantry), who gave it to the Bersaglieri as a gift for their bravery.

The fez was worn in place of the *bustina* by other ranks and NCOs in the barracks or during field training.

The Arditi fez was similar to the Bersaglieri design, though it was all black – adopted from Italian World War I assault soldiers – and was normal headwear for all MVSN ranks up to corporal-major. Other ranks and NCOs of the Young Fascist Regiment also wore this black pattern. This fez was worn with pride by all who were entitled to it.

All ranks of the Fascist Albanian Militia wore a white round Muslim fez without a tassel. A stamped metal MVSN badge, which had a central fascio flanked by a wreath and topped with a five-pointed star, was sewn on to the front of the fez.

Two Bersaglieri wearing their red fez with blue tassel work on a truck engine in the vicinity of the Egyptian front, 13 September 1942. (Rudy D'Angelo)

Chapter Five
Small-Arms and Field Equipment

Artillery Service

THE STUDY, production, supply, maintenance, storage and distribution of heavy and light arms, ammunition and explosives was the function of the Artillery Service. In 1939 the following installations were supplying the service with arms and material:

(1) Three army arsenals at Naples, Turin and Piacenza for the manufacture and repair of guns, carriages, projectiles and ordnance equipment.

(2) A small-arms manufacturing plant at Terni in central Italy, with a subsidiary plant at Gardone in the north.

(3) Two small-arms ammunition plants at Capua and Bologna.

(4) A fuse-manufacturing plant at Rome, with a subsidiary plant at Torre Annunziata in the south.

(5) A powder plant at Fontana Liri in the south.

(6) A plant at Rome for the manufacture of optical and fire-control instruments.

(7) A laboratory at Piacenza for loading artillery projectiles.

(8) A projectile plant at Genoa.

Method of Supply

The system of requisition of ammunition and supplies was as follows. For small-arms, infantry-accompanying guns and hand grenades, requisitions were submitted by regimental headquarters through divisional HQ to corps HQ, where they were consolidated by the corps general staff and forwarded to the army directorate.

For artillery, they were passed from batteries through regimental headquarters to corps artillery, where they were consolidated and forwarded to army administration, which arranged for supplies.

The distribution points were determined by the army administration but were organised by the chiefs of staff and artillery headquarters of smaller units. They were located within convenient distance of the army depot and close to good roads where possible, so as to be easily reached by truck convoys provided by the Transport Service directorate at army HQ. Transportation from the distributing posts was supplied by the divisions and other units requiring it.

This system was quite flexible. Commanders of front-line soldiers could request ammunition from nearby posts if necessary, or headquarters of large units could request supplies directly from the army directorate without passing through the usual channels.

Maintenance and minor repairs were carried out by camp workshops. Heavier repairs were undertaken at base workshops.

In dealing with the subject of weapons in the Italian army one is confronted with an extraordinary multiplicity of types and a variety of deployment. Obsolete models still in use, and the Italian aptitude for improvisation, are reflected in the number of dual-purpose weapons. Those discussed here are the standard-issue small-arms and some infantry-accompanying guns which were used extensively by the army.

All Italian artillery was distinguished by two numbers separated by an oblique stroke. The first number indicates the calibre in millimetres; the second gives the length of the bore in calibres. Equipment was classified as: Gun – bore longer than 22 calibres; Howitzer – bore between 12 and 22 calibres; Mortar – bore shorter than 12 calibres.

Benito Mussolini reviews a line-up of M35 20/65 20mm Breda anti-aircraft guns. (Author's collection)

Model 35, 20/65 AA Gun (Breda)

This gun was a 20 mm gas-operated dual-purpose anti-aircraft or anti-tank weapon, with a course and speed sight. It could be drawn by motor transport or in four pack-loads, and was served by three gunners.

Fed by plate charges holding twelve rounds each (tracer or armour piercing rounds could be used), a continuous rate of fire (approximately 120 rounds a minute) could be obtained by loading a further plate charge immediately after the preceding one. However, the small size of the magazine was a disadvantage.

The weapon was normally employed for anti-aircraft defence and in Libya was devastating against low-flying aircraft, although with a range of only 2,300 metres it was ineffective against high-flying craft. Occasionally it was used as an anti-tank weapon, though only over short distances. Members of the Australian 3rd Light Anti-Aircraft Regiment used captured examples of these guns with great effect in and around Fort Pilastrino, Tobruk, Libya, during 1941.

Model 37, 47/32 Anti-Tank Gun

This 47 mm anti-tank gun was basically a good weapon boasting a high rate of fire, and could be used either on wheels or from its platform. It could also be used as an infantry-support gun, though the high explosive charge was relatively erratic in performance compared with its armour-piercing shell. It had a practical rate of fire of seven to eight rounds per minute.

The gun could be transported by manpower, with the use of special ropes, drawn by a mule or a truck, or divided into five pack-loads.

Its disadvantages were that no protection was provided for the crew, the traverse was limited and the hitting power was inferior to that of the British two-pounder. Because of its poor performance against Allied armour in North Africa, it was not a popular gun with its crew. The 26th Australian Anti-Tank Company was issued captured 47/32 A-T guns at Tobruk as no British guns were available. About half of the 113 anti-tank guns used around Tobruk by the Australians in 1941 were captured Italian weapons.

A crew of a dug in M37 47/32 anti-tank gun fire off a round. North Africa 1942. (Bundesarchiv, Koblenz)

65/17 Infantry Gun

The 65 mm infantry gun was an obsolete weapon of World War I vintage, being an adaptation of the Italian-made 65 mm mountain gun. For mobility the 65/17 was provided with a fore-carriage. It was easy to dismantle so it could be carried by mules.

The 65/17 fired three kinds of projectiles: H.E. shell,

A soldier sights on a target while the rest of the crew prepares to load a round into a 65/17 infantry gun. North Africa. (Otto Meyer)

armour-piercing shell and grapeshot. Its rate of fire was six to eight rounds per minute, with a maximum range of 6,500 metres. It was considered a good weapon, accurate over a straight though short range.

Mortars

Model 35, 81 mm

This was the army's standard medium mortar, similar to the British three-inch one. It was a smooth-bore, muzzle-loading weapon of conventional design. It fired two types of high-explosive bombs, a light one of 3.402 kg and a heavy one of 6.804 kg. The fragmentation of both types was relatively ineffective.

Chemical bombs used by the chemical mortar battalions fired a bomb weighing approximately 3 kg.

The mortars, although excellent for mountain warfare, were found to be of almost no use in the desert and were sent back to the arsenals.

Infantry of the Bologna infantry division with an 81 mm model 35 mortar. Libya 1942. (Author's collection)

Model 35, 45 mm (Brixia)

This was the standard light mortar – a breech-loaded, trigger-fired weapon with high and low capabilities.

This complex weapon had a number of good points, including a high rate of fire (twenty-five to thirty rounds per minute), steadiness in action and the fact that it folded conveniently for carrying. These advantages had, however, only been obtained at the expense of an unusually elaborate design, and were largely offset by the poor fragmentation of the mortar bomb, which weighed 453 grammes.

Hand Grenades

Three models of hand grenades were in general service use – the OTO Model 35, SRCM M35 and the Breda M35. These were very light metal grenades of similar construction (weighing approximately 3 kg). Only in the case of the SRCM was there any metal-loading fragmentation or anti-personnel effect.

Reliance was placed mainly on blast, which was fair, with a good deal of smoke and noise.

Model 35 Brixia 45mm light mortar.

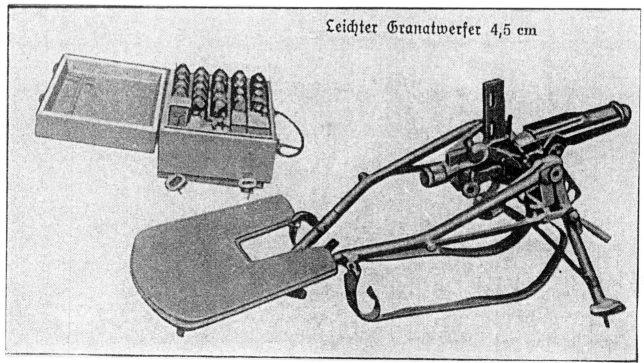

Grenades are issued to infantry before a patrol. Tobruk, North Africa 1941. (Author's collection)

All were armed and fired in the same manner. They were grasped in the right hand and the rubber tab was pulled away with the left. The grenade was then thrown in the usual manner, and detonated on impact with the ground – mostly. . . .

The trio were given the name 'Red Devils' by Allied soldiers because of their colour and the fact that many unsuspecting soldiers picked them up unexploded, triggering the detonators, with nasty results! These hand grenades were reissued to British soldiers fighting the Vichy French during the Syrian campaign of June 1941, from Italian stocks captured in Eritrea.

A flare is taped on to a Molotov cocktail. It was used as a fuse on the cocktail by artillery troops in the vicinity of Tobruk, North Africa. November 1941. (Author's collection)

A profusion of small-arms and grenades dropped by surrendering Italian soldiers, trapped after crossing the salt marsh near the coast road between Bugbug and Sollum in Egypt, North Africa 1941. (Author's collection)

Revolvers and Pistols

Pistols were used extensively by the Italian army – they were standard issue to officers, some NCOs, armoured crews, transport drivers and soldiers on special duty. Air force and navy officers and NCOs also carried side-arms. Arms factories were hard pressed to produce pistols in sufficient numbers and so a variety of obsolete side-arms were retained to fill the gap between supply and demand.

Model 1889 Glisenti Revolver

The model 1889 was a double-action revolver known as the Bodeo system, of solid frame and rather old-fashioned design. Although reliable enough it did have several faults. The six-shot cylinder did not swing out and empty cases could only be removed singly by the ejection rod. The 10.35 mm calibre cartridge was underpowered in comparison to its size, although at the short range at which pistols were normally used this did not make much difference to its performance in comparison with other side-arms. It had a length of 23.45 cm.

Several variations were produced. One version for other ranks had an octagonal barrel and an unusual trigger without a guard which could swing shut under the pistol when not in use. There was also a version for officers with the same specifications as the other ranks' type, except that it had a more conventional trigger and guard, and initially was better finished. This quality disappeared with the high volume of manufacture during World War I. In later years the pistols were known as Type A and B, with no distinction as to who used them.

Produced at the same time was a variation known as Light Type 1889, introduced because the previous types were considered too heavy and cumbersome (although they were nevertheless still used). This pistol had a round barrel with a conventional trigger and guard, and was shorter, 20.93 cm long. In all other specifications it was much the same as its forerunners.

These pistols continued to be manufactured throughout the 1920s. All types saw service during World War II by the native colonial soldiers, though not by regular army or MVSN formations. Its popularity waned as ammunition became difficult to obtain. It was one of the oldest service hand-guns still in use by a European-led army during World War II.

PISTOLA AUTOMATICA BERETTA CALIBRO 9

SCALA 2:1

SEZIONI LONGITUDINALI DEL MECCANISMO DI CARICAMENTO E SPARO - ARMA CARICA -

PERCUSSIONE DELLÀ CARTUCCIA

PRONTA PER LO SPARO

PERCUSSIONE E SPARO - ARMA CARICA -

VISTA DI FIANCO

VISTA DI FIANCO IN POSIZ. DI SICUR.

POSIZIONE DI MASSIMO RINCULO

CULATTA-OTTURATORE APERTA CON AVVISO DI CARICATORE VUOTO

VISTA DI SOPRA

PESO Kg. 0.880

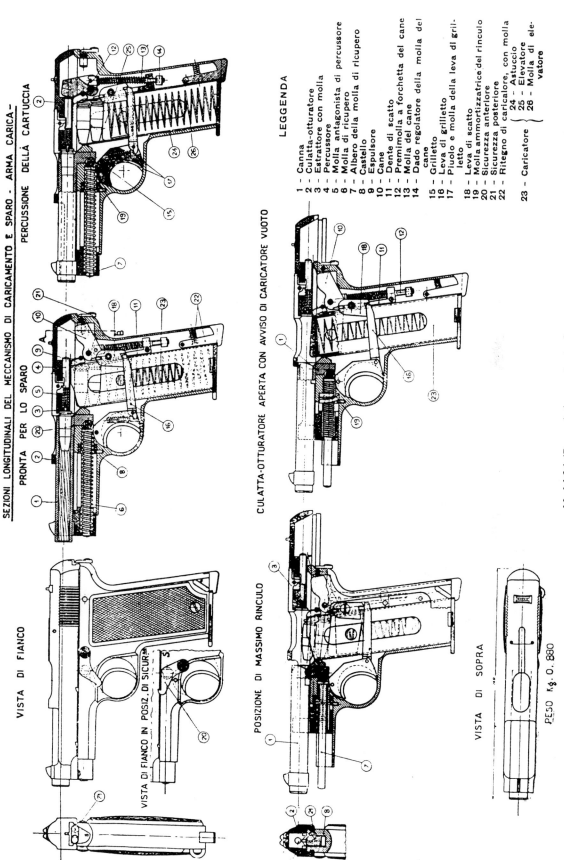

LEGGENDA

1 - Canna
2 - Culatta-otturatore
3 - Estrattore con molla
4 - Percussore
5 - Molla antagonista di percussore
6 - Molla di ricupero
7 - Albero della molla di ricupero
8 - Castello
9 - Espulsore
10 - Cane
11 - Dente di scatto
12 - Premimolla a forchetta del cane
13 - Molla del cane
14 - Dado regolatore della molla del cane
15 - Grilletto
16 - Leva di grilletto
17 - Piuolo e molla della leva di grilletto
18 - Leva di scatto
19 - Molla ammortizzatrice del rinculo
20 - Sicurezza anteriore
21 - Sicurezza posteriore
22 - Ritegno di caricalore, con molla
23 - Caricatore
24 - Astuccio
25 - Elevatore
26 - Molla di elevatore

Model 34 (Beretta) Automatic pistol.

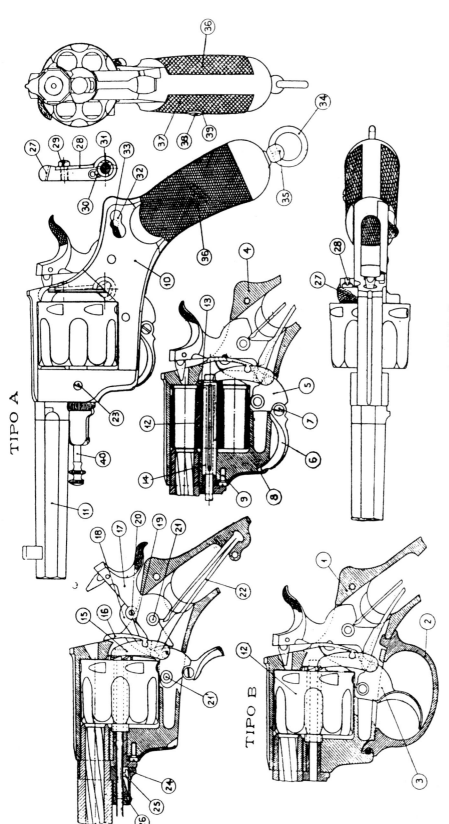

PISTOLA A ROTAZIONE MOD. 1889

TIPO A

TIPO B

PARTI COMUNI ALLE DUE PISTOLE

Model 1889 Glisenti Revolver.

PARTI DI PISTOLA (TIPO B)

1 – Castello
2 – Ponticello
3 – Grilletto

PARTI DI PISTOLA (TIPO A)

4 – Castello
5 – Grilletto
6 – Coda di grilletto

7 – Vite di coda di grilletto
8 – Molla-ritegno di coda di grilletto
9 – Vite di molla-ritegno di coda di grilletto
10 – Cartella
11 – Canna
12 – Cilindro
13 – Tubicino dentiera
14 – Albero, con molla
15 – Bocciuolo
16 – Cuneo di sicurezza
17 – Cane

18 – Appendice di cane
19 – Molletta di appendice
20 – Vite-perno di appendice di cane
21 – Perno del cane
21[1] – Perno del grilletto
22 – Mollone
23 – Vite ritegno di albero
24 – Ghiera porta bacchetta
25 – Molletta di bacchetta
26 – Vite di molletta di bacchetta
27 – Sportello
28 – Molla di sportello

29 – Vite di molla di sportello
30 – Piuolo di sportello, con vite
31 – Perno dello sportello
32 – Vite di cartella
33 – Vite prigioniera di vite di cartella
34 – Campanella
35 – Porta campanella, con dado
36 – Guancia sinistra
37 – Guancia destra
38 – Vite di guancia
39 – Rosetta
40 – Bocchetta

116

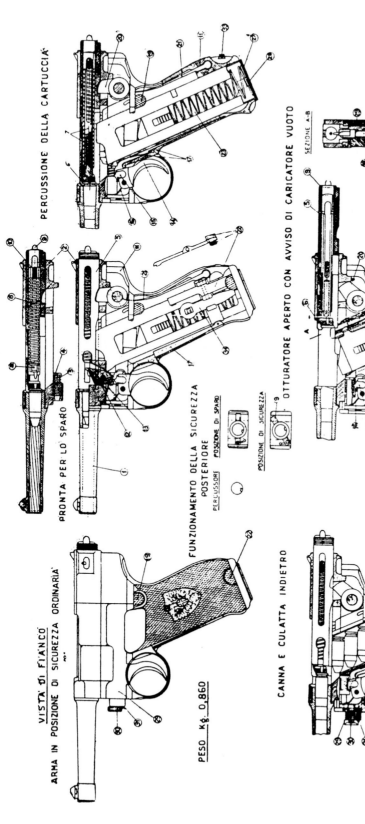

PISTOLA AUTOMATICA MOD. 910 CALIBRO 9

TAV. 9

SEZIONI LONGITUDINALI DEL MECCANISMO DI CARICAMENTO E SPARO – ARMA CARICA

PERCUSSIONE DELLA CARTUCCIA

PRONTA PER LO SPARO

FUNZIONAMENTO DELLA SICUREZZA POSTERIORE

PERCUSSORE POSIZIONE DI SPARO

PERCUSSORE POSIZIONE DI SICUREZZA

OTTURATORE APERTO CON AVVISO DI CARICATORE VUOTO

SEZIONE A-B

VISTA DI FIANCO

ARMA IN POSIZIONE DI SICUREZZA ORDINARIA

PESO Kg. 0,860

CANNA E CULATTA INDIETRO

SEZIONE ORIZZONTALE SULL'ASSE DELL'OTTURATORE

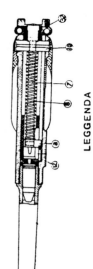

LEGGENDA

1 - Canna
2 - Culatta
3 - Molla ricuperatrice di culatta
4 - Alberello di molla ricuperatrice di culatta
5 - Otturatore
6 - Estrattore
7 - Percussore con dente d'arresto (a)
8 - Molla spirale di percussore
9 - Sicurezza posteriore
10 - Chiavetta con molla d'arresto
11 - Castello
12 - Leva di scatto con perno
13 - Molla di leva di scatto con vite
14 - Grilletto
15 - Dente di scappamento
16 - Molla di grilletto e di dente di scappamento
17 - Sicurezza anteriore con molla
18 - Espulsore con molla
19 - Leva d'espulsore

20 - Blocco di chiusura
21 - Molla del blocco di chiusura
22 - Ritegno di caricatore con molla e perno
23 - Caricatore
 24 - Astuccio
 25 - Elevatore
 26 - Molla di elevatore
 27 - Fondello del caricatore
 28 - Piastrina di ritegno del fondello
29 - Cartella
30 - Vite della cartella con testa godronata
31 - Piuolo di ritegno della vite della cartella con molla e tappetto a vite
32 - Piuolo d'arresto della sicurezza posteriore, con molla
33 - Traversino dell'impugnatura
34 - Cacciavite

Model 1910 Automatic pistol.

117

Model 1910 Automatic Pistol

Although known officially as the Glisenti Automatic Pistol, this was produced by two manufacturers, Glisenti of Turin and Brixia of Brescia, one of the largest industrial and arsenal cities in northern Italy. Although both pistols superficially resembled the German Luger, the mechanism was quite different, and the 9 mm-calibre cartridge less powerful than the Luger round. The chamber would accept the parabellum round, although it was not considered at all safe to fire the more powerful ammunition in the Model 1910.

Both pistols were 20.6 cm long and had a seven-shot butt-loaded magazine. The Brixia version differed from the Glisenti mainly in minor features which did not change the basic structure or operation. Some parts were thicker, increasing the general weight, and the Brixia had a safety catch which stopped the pistol being fired after the magazine had been removed.

The left side of the frame had a detachable plate which was good for access to clean the internals but lessened the strength of the frame – the plate had a disturbing habit of coming loose with the vibration of shooting.

The M1910 was originally issued as an officers' side-arm and first used during the 1911 Libyan war. It remained the official side-arm until it was replaced by the Model 34 Beretta. Although its production and use continued during World War II it was mainly issued to Carabinieri, reserve and non-combatant units. Some officers had a preference for the 'Luger-look' of the Glisenti, even if the Beretta was superior in performance.

Model 34 (Beretta) Automatic Pistol

The model 1934 Beretta was a small, robust, functional, reliable and very well-made automatic pistol with an external hammer, a fixed barrel and a recoiling breech-slide. It was 15 cm in length, fired a 9 mm short cartridge which was rather underpowered for military use, and had a seven-round, butt-loaded magazine.

A popular pistol, it was by far the best sidearm issued to the Italian military. It was very popular with the Italians and a much-prized souvenir among Allied soldiers. The Germans also admired it and after 1943 took over the Beretta factories and used the output for their own personnel. It is not surprising, then, that it was standard issue for the Italian army throughout the 1930s and World War II.

Machine-Guns

Model 30 (Breda)

The Breda company of Brescia had been a locomotive-manufacturing concern before branching out into the arms field, initially as a sub-contractor to Fiat during World War I. The first machine-gun designed and built wholly by Breda was the Model 30, which became the main light machine-gun of the Italian army. It was a bipod-mounted, gas-operated, air-cooled weapon with interchangeable barrels (an innovation at the time) which needed to be changed after 250 rounds of rapid fire. The fitted magazine swung forward to take strips of twenty rounds of 6.5 mm calibre – the same ammunition as that used in the Carcano rifles. The rounds were lubricated with an oil pump before chambering, the idea being that the oil facilitated the smooth passage of the cartridge. It had a maximum rate of fire of 400 to 500 rounds per minute.

The Model 30 gained a deservedly bad reputation for reliability – it easily clogged with dirt and sand because the lubricating oil picked up grit which acted as an abrasive, causing stoppages. The 6.5 mm round was underpowered, the fixed bipod made it undesirable for long-range work and on rough ground it was impossible to keep upright. There was no provision for the carrying handle, so the gunner had to carry the often hot gun as best he could. It was promptly discarded by the Italians in North Africa when they captured large supplies of British Bren machine-guns. It did, however, continue to be used on all fronts on which the Italians fought.

Model 37 (Breda)

This was a tripod-mounted, gas-operated, air-cooled medium machine-gun, also with interchangeable barrels. The 8 mm-calibre rounds were fed into the breech by a flat tray of twenty rounds. An unusual feed system saw the spent cases returned to the tray, which was only ejected after all the rounds had been fired, the idea being that the cases could be retrieved for reloading.

The sad truth was, however, that many were damaged during ejection, making the whole exercise rather pointless. The 'official' maximum rate of fire of 450 rounds per minute would have been somewhat reduced as the small ammunition clips made continuous firing difficult to maintain.

BREDA mod. 30

FUCILE MITRAGLIATORE

1. Testata con calcio - 2. Castello - 3. Bipide - 4. Canna - 5. Mirino - 6. Piastra di bloccaggio - 7. Blocco giunto - 8. Otturatore - 9. Percussore con molla - 10. Serbatoio cartucce - 11. Alzo - 12. Sicurezza a mano - 13. Carrello d'armamento - 14. Espulsore - 15. Perno della scatola del lubrificante - 16. Chiavistello - 17. Scatola del lubrificante - 18. Mollone dell'otturatore - 19. Chiera guida - 20. Mollone ammortizzatore del rinculo - 21. Bocchetto - 22. Apertura del bocchetto di caricamento..

Model 30 (Breda) machine-gun.

Blackshirt Francesco Breschi (centre) fires a Breda M30 light machine-gun in Ethiopia, 1936. (Carlo Breschi)

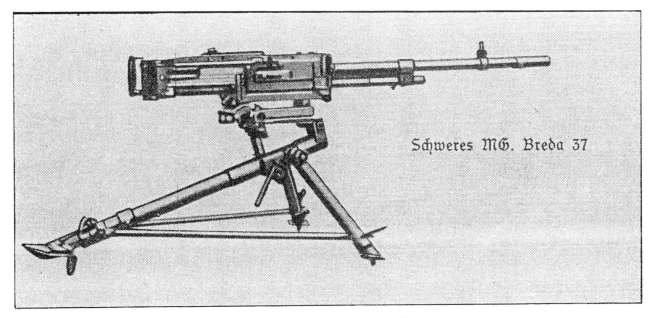

Schweres MG. Breda 37

The model 37 (Breda) 8mm medium machine-gun.

A member of the Giovani Fascisti regiment cleans the mechanism of a Fiat M35 8mm machine-gun. Tunisia, North Africa. April 1943. (Bundesarchiv, Koblenz)

In spite of this the Model 37 had a reputation for being reliable and was considered the army's best machine-gun. The Australian troops in Tobruk in 1941 admired it and used captured examples against their former owners. The Model 37 served faithfully on all war fronts.

Model 14 (Fiat–Revelli)

This water-cooled tripod medium weapon was originally used during World War I (it resembled the German Maxim machine-gun) and saw service until the end of World War II. It was fed by a box of 6.5 mm rounds divided into ten compartments of five rounds each. Each round was oiled by a reservoir as it entered the chamber but, as with the M30 Breda, grit accumulated in the various exposed parts, causing stoppages for which it was noted. This drawback made it unpopular with its crew.

For such a bulky and complicated gun its 400 rounds per minute rate of fire was disappointing, particularly when coupled with the underpowered 6.5 mm round.

Model 35 (Fiat–Revelli)

Designed as a replacement for the Model 14 6.5 mm – some of which were converted to M35s – this had a tripod and anti-aircraft mounting and the water-cooled barrel was swapped for a quick-change air-cooled type.

The box magazine was sometimes replaced with a belt feed and in some cases was upgraded to 8 mm calibre to improve its hitting power.

These improvements still left a gun which was not totally satisfactory. The gun was prone to 'cook' rounds in the chamber through the heat generated from the light air-cooled barrel. It had a rate of fire of 225 to 450 rpm, depending on whether or not a declarator was fitted to the barrel.

Model 38A Moschetto Automatico Beretta (MAB)

The Model 38A MAB was the only submachine-gun used by the Italian forces in any quantity throughout World War II and was considered above average, both in function and in convenience of handling. Early models had a short, folding bayonet fitted under the barrel jacket. It fired a 9 mm-long parabellum round and used either a 10, 20 or 40-round box magazine.

An unusual trigger mechanism meant the M38A could fire both single and automatic fire – the front trigger for single rounds and the rear for automatic; the rear trigger was provided with a plunger which locked, preventing inadvertent automatic fire. Maximum rate of fire was 600 rounds per minute.

In 1942 a modified version of the M38A known as the M38A/42 was introduced. It retained the basic mechanism and outline of the M38A, although stamped steel parts were used to reduce manufacture time with little loss of quality. Maximum rate of fire was 550 rpm.

Captured M38As were used by the Allies in North Africa for raiding parties where a light weapon with a high rate of fire power was required. The Germans also respected the MAB and used large numbers in Italy after 1943.

Infantry soldiers use a Fiat-Revelli model 1914 machine-gun on an anti-aircraft mounting on manoeuvres in Sicily. (Author's collection)

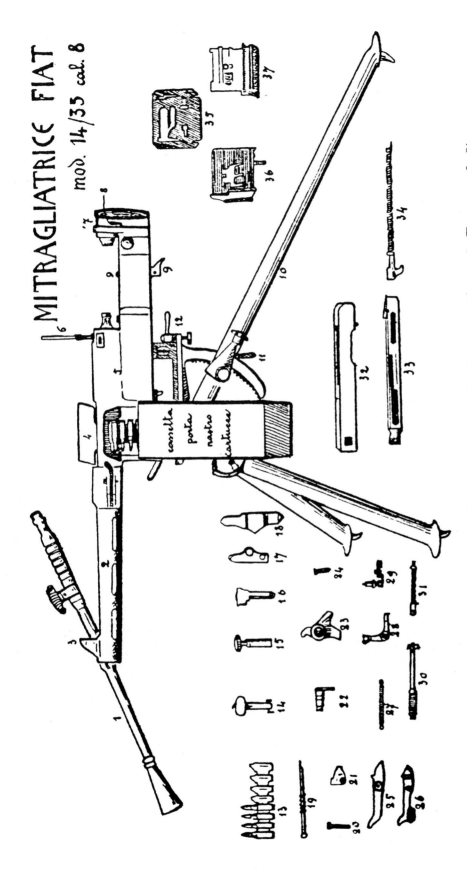

MITRAGLIATRICE FIAT
mod. 14/35 cal. 8

comma porta nastro cartucce

1. Canna — 2. Manicotto — 3. Mirino — 4. Sportello a cerniera — 5. Castello — 6. Alzo — 7. Testata — 8. Sicurezza a mano — 9. Congegno d'arresto dell'otturatore — 10. Treppiede — 11. Morsetto di bloccaggio limitatore del traballamento — 12. Settore di falciamento con bottone limitatore e morsetto di bloccaggio — 13. Nasto metallico con cartucce — 14. Leva di sparo — 15. Chiavistello — 16. Chiavetta — 17. Controleva di alimentazione — 18. Leva di alimentazione — 19. Asta di scatto — 20. Bottone di rcatto — 21. Grilletto — 22. Perno di blocco — 23. Blocco — 24. Perno della leva di scatto — 25. Leva di scatto di sinistra — 26. Leva di scatto di destra — 27. Molla a spirale di alimentazicne — 28. Spostatore — 29. Penno del destro spostatore — 30. Tirante del blocco — 31. Asticolo con molla di richiamo del carrello — 32. Culatta mobile — 33. Otturatore — 34. Percursore — 35. Cartella di destra — 36. Telaio con cartella di sinistra e carrello d'alimentazione — 37. Bocchetto d'alimentazione.

Model 35 (Fiat-Revelli) machine-gun.

Rifles

The bolt-action rifles used by the Italian army were of an old design predating World War I. There were two basic types of long arm – the rifle and the shorter carbine, which had two variations. One was known as the TS – for use by gunners, signalmen and other such specialists; the second variation had a spike bayonet permanently attached to the muzzle which could be folded back when not in use. This type was issued to cavalry, paratroops and Carabinieri mounted.

The rifles had straight bolt handles while the carbines had a downward-facing handle originally designed so it could be placed in a saddle holster. The rifle and carbine both underwent a series of revisions throughout their service lives, but the basic concept was retained and all looked virtually the same.

The basic Mannlicher-Carcano concept embodied in all Italian rifles and carbines stemmed from the original 1891 design and combined the Mannlicher system of clip-loading with a bolt action of the Mauser-type. All Carcanos were single-fire weapons which initially held a clip of six rounds of 6.5 mm calibre in the magazine. The six-round clip was not considered large enough, but there was no way of improving the design of the rifle to increase the amount of rounds held in the clip.

In 1937 the military authorities decided to replace the underpowered 6.5 mm round with the more powerful 7.35 mm calibre. Production began on the new calibre and associated weapons but with World War II looming there was insufficient time to complete the programme and it was abandoned. The outcome was that both the 6.5 mm and 7.65 mm calibres were used on all fronts by the army. In Russia, after the first year of the campaign, the 7.35 mm calibre weapons were sent back and exchanged for the 6.5 mm version.

The Model 38 short rifle, TS carbine and cavalry carbine designed for the new calibre were made in 7.35 mm through to 1940, at which time production was switched back to 6.5 mm for all models, the reason being a shortage of 7.35 mm ammunition. Soldiers on the North African and Greek fronts continued to use both types until the end.

Italy also produced the TS and cavalry carbines in 8 mm in small numbers from 1938–9. Then in 1941 20,000 were ordered from arms manufacturers RE Terni and FNA-Brescia. Intended for service on the

Ascari with Carcano M91 rifles and bayonets dance around their commanding officer before a military operation. Ethiopia 1936. (Author's collection)

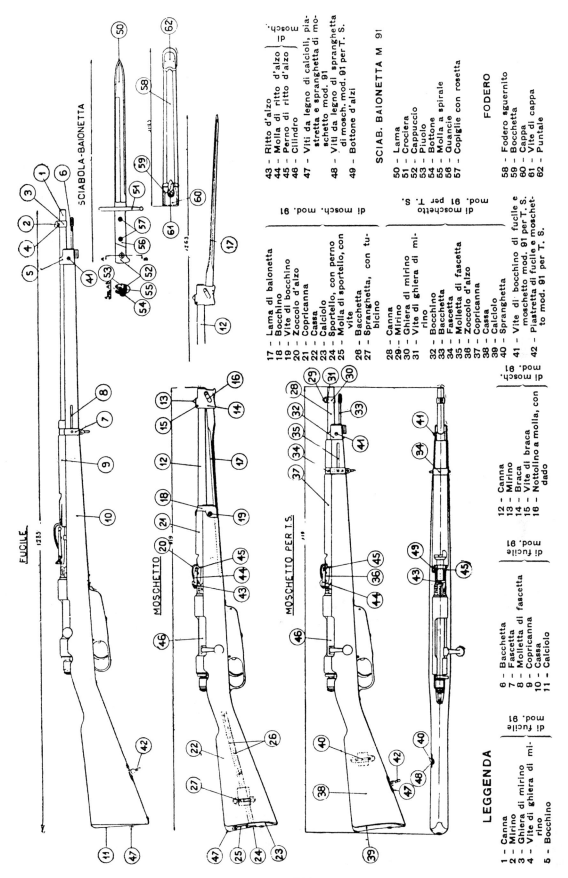

ARMI MOD. 91

FUCILE

SCIABOLA-BAIONETTA

MOSCHETTO

MOSCHETTO PER T.S.

SCIAB. BAIONETTA M 91

FODERO

LEGGENDA

1 – Canna
2 – Mirino
3 – Ghiera di mirino
4 – Vite di ghiera di mirino
5 – Bocchino
6 – Bacchetta
7 – Fascetta
8 – Molletta di fascetta
9 – Copricanna
10 – Cassa
11 – Calciolo

12 – Canna
13 – Mirino
14 – Braca
15 – Vite di braca
16 – Nottolino a molla, con dado

17 – Lama di baionetta
18 – Bocchino
19 – Vite di bocchino
20 – Zoccolo d'alzo
21 – Copricanna
22 – Cassa
23 – Calciolo
24 – Sportello, con perno
25 – Molla di sportello, con vite
26 – Bacchetta
27 – Spranghetta, con tubicino

28 – Canna
29 – Mirino
30 – Ghiera di mirino
31 – Vite di ghiera di mirino
32 – Bocchino
33 – Bacchetta
34 – Fascetta
35 – Molletta di fascetta
36 – Zoccolo d'alzo
37 – Copricanna
38 – Cassa
39 – Calciolo
40 – Spranghetta
41 – Vite di bocchino di fucile e moschetto mod. 91 per T. S.
42 – Piastretta di fucile e moschetto mod. 91 per T. S.

43 – Ritto d'alzo
44 – Molla di ritto d'alzo
45 – Perno di ritto d'alzo
46 – Cilindro
47 – Viti da legno di calcioli, piastretta e spranghetta di moschetto mod. 91
48 – Viti da legno di spranghetta di mosch. mod. 91 per T. S.
49 – Bottone d'alzi

50 – Lama
51 – Crociera
52 – Cappuccio
53 – Piuolo
54 – Bottone
55 – Molla a spirale
56 – Quancie
57 – Copiglie con rosetta

58 – Fodero sguernito
59 – Bocchetta
60 – Cappa
61 – Vite di cappa
62 – Puntale

Model 91 Carcano rifle and carbine.

Russian front, they were not widely used as the recoil was reported to be most brutal.

The Germans took over supplies of Carcanos in 1943 for issue to their own units in Italy. In 1944 some were rebored to the German 7.92 mm calibre which would have been at the limit the Carcano could have been bored – as it was the rifle was not considered entirely safe to fire in that calibre.

A specially made scaled-down version of the Model 91 carbine (known as the Balilla regulation musket Model 1891 reduced) was used by the Fascist Youth authorities as a training weapon. Some 30,000 were made by FNA during the 1930s. This smooth-bore carbine fired a 5.5 mm blank cartridge held in a six-shot clip. A blunted folding bayonet was attached.

The many varied calibres of revolver, pistol, rifle, submachine-gun and machine-gun cartridges used by the Italians were at times a nightmare for supply authorities.

Bayonets and Combat Daggers

The official side-arm worn by other ranks of the Royal Army was the bayonet. These were found in several types and variations, the standard being the Carcano M1891 knife bayonet used on 1891 system rifles and carbines. This had a steel hilt with a straight mortise slot and a press-locking stud, a straight steel cross-guard with a muzzle ring and wooden hand-grips secured by two rivets. The blade was of a straight single-edged fullered pattern.

Two types of scabbard were used – a black leather one with brass mountings and a scarcer steel fluted version. Both had a frog stud for affixing to the grey-green leather scabbard. Overall length of the bayonet was 41.4 cm.

A bayonet was introduced in 1938 for use on the MAB 38A, but because of the barrel jacket size no muzzle ring was used. Instead, a stud was fixed on to a mortise slot on the underside of the barrel.

The hilt was steel, the hand-grips were wood secured by two rivets and the steel blade was a straight single-edged type which could be folded back on to the handle or locked into an open position. A non-folding rigid type was also made.

The scabbards were steel, some with a metal loop for wearing on the belt without a leather frog. Others had a frog stud for wearing with an M91 leather frog.

Overall bayonet length was 30.7 cm and 31.1 cm respectively.

In the same year a bayonet similar in appearance to the MAB 38 pattern was introduced for M1891/38 system rifles and carbines. The difference was that the rifle bayonet had a muzzle ring, although a folding blade was again used, the intent being for it to be carried on the rifle at all times, with the blade folded when not in use. However, this was not successful, as the blades became loose and lost their rigidity.

The problem was remedied by having the blades fixed rigidly and using a new steel crossguard. The steel MAB 38A bayonet scabbards were used. Overall length was 28.8 cm.

A combination bayonet/entrenching-tool carrier in grey-green or green-brown leather was worn on the belt and included a section for the entrenching tool. Fastened directly on to the front was a separate frog carrier for the M91 or M38 bayonet. A strap stitched to the back flap was used to secure the tool.

A number of entrenching tools were worn in this combination, including:

(1) A field shovel known as the Model 1907. This was a well-made and sturdy tool, with a reinforced spine. Holes on either side of the tool head were used to secure it when it was carried in the combination frog carrier. The steel was of blackened iron and the handle was wood.

(2) Infantry pick-axe. This was used by infantry, Alpini and Bersaglieri, and had a black hardened steel head of which one end was a pick and the other an axe, with a wooden handle. It was a good, strong tool and was carried on the belt or on the knapsack.

(3) The infantry pick-axe and entrenching tool also had a blackened steel head which was a hoe with a reinforced central ridge at one end and an axe at the other. It was carried in the combination frog carrier.

(4) A tool used by the Alpini for mountain scaling was also carried by infantry-engineers and Bersaglieri. The steel head had a pick at one end and a flat hoe at the other. This too was carried in the combination frog carrier.

The dagger was the official side-arm used by Fascist Militia and was worn by all ranks in various forms. In 1925 a dagger was introduced for wear by MVSN NCOs and officers and for the Colonial Blackshirt Militia. It was adopted by the National Paratroop Battalion of Libya in the late 1930s for wear by its troopers and Italian officers. The black wooden grips of ebony, dark ash or dark walnut had a brass *fascio* inset into the handle on both sides. A cast steel pommel surmounted the handle, while a straight steel crossguard with ball-terminated quillions was fixed to the base of the handle. On the front plate of the crossguard was stamped MVSN, while on the reverse was a stamped letter and serial number.

The blade was made from cut-down M1887 Vetterli-Vitali socket bayonets which had a cruciform blade ending in a sharp point. The scabbard was oval-shaped black painted steel, with a large steel belt loop on the reverse. Overall length with scabbard was 33.5 cm.

The first true combat dagger for Fascist Militia other ranks and officers was introduced in 1935. It was of sturdy construction, and the plain wooden handle was contoured with four finger grooves. Two rivets secured the blade tang to the handle and the pommel had a steel cap.

The crossguard was steel, with a single upswept quillion. The broad steel blade had a central spine which ran down its length, with a cutting edge 18 cm long on one side and a false edge 14 cm long from the tip on the other.

The pressed steel scabbard was painted black and featured an embossed *fascio* and the initials MVSN for other ranks. On the rear was a rigid steel angled belt loop.

The NCOs' and officers' model was almost identical in design but was of a better grade of steel, with blued metal fittings and nickel rivets. NCOs' had grips made of high-quality wood such as mahogany and cherry, while officers had grips of black ebony. Generals had grips of ivory – the mark of high rank. All metal parts for generals' daggers, including the blade, were of chrome or nickel.

The officers' scabbards were plain black and not embossed, as some units of the army wore this dagger as well and technically owed allegiance to the Crown, not to the Fascist party. On the rear of the scabbard was a vertical swivel belt loop which could be slid open to fit over the belt without removing it from the trousers. Generals, however, had an embossed scabbard with the *fascio* and letters MVSN, though with officers' fixtures. Overall length with scabbard for all patterns was 33.5 cm.

A second pattern of combat knife introduced in 1939 was widely used by paratroops, MVSN Blackshirt and assault units, Fascist Youth combat units within the army, Fascist Albanian Militia and Libyan units attached to the Colonial Army. The wooden handle was rounded and slightly longer. Officers often had a superior quality wooden handle affixed, while general had ivory grips. Three rivets secured the blade tang to the handle, an oval steel crossguard replaced the upturned steel guard, while a sharper and higher quality steel blade replaced the rather cruder first pattern version. The blade had an 18 cm cutting edge and a false edge extending 9 cm from the tip. It was designed specifically for killing.

The scabbard was the same as the M35 type and painted black, though without any *fascio* or initials, since army as well as Militia officers preferred to carry this model in the field. However, many Blackshirts favoured the first model scabbard and thus both types were worn. A swivelled metal belt loop was attached to the rear. Overall length with scabbard was 33.5 cm.

Many daggers are found that have carved handles with the names of wives, girlfriends, children, units, campaigns, dates of combat, home towns and unit mottoes, as well as Fascist, Nazi or Alliance symbols and motifs. This was common practice among the Italian soldiers with artistic talent.

The cavalry of the Italian army wore a sabre as part of its combat equipment, not merely as a ceremonial side-arm. The cavalry model of 1873 was the regulation edged weapon for officers of the cavalry, lancers and light cavalry. It was similar to the field sabre used by officers in the US army. The sabre featured all nickelled parts and a guard with three branches. The grips were of black ebony without finger grooves, although generals and colonels in command had theirs made of ivory or a composite of ground ivory called *ivorine*. During the later stages of World War II grips were made of hard plastic or bakelite.

Blades were engraved with a variety of military motifs, but the main feature was usually the crowned Eagle of Savoy on one side and the crest of the House of Savoy on the other. Swords with Damascus blades were also ordered by generals and noblemen in the ranks and those on whom the king had bestowed orders of chivalry. A green leather sword knot was worn in the field, and brown leather ones by officers in the Colonies. The metal scabbard always had two carrying rings.

A variety of arsenals and manufacturing firms made these swords for all ranks. Some German firms from Soligen were also on contract to the Italians.

The Model 1871 sabre for cavalry other ranks was all steel, and sported a large, wide basket guard with a single large teardrop section. It had a straight wooden grip of various shades – from light brown to almost black. The blade for other ranks was heavy, sturdy and without engraving and the steel scabbard had a single carrying ring. It was worn with the uniform or on the saddle when the soldier was on horseback. Swords and scabbards usually had the same issue number.

Warrant officers of mounted units wore the Model 1871/29 sabre, which was modified in 1929 from the Model 1871 version worn by other ranks (the modification consisted of the addition of an extra scabbard ring). The sabre had a large basket, a large teardrop section and natural wood grips.

Total length of 1871 and 1871/29 pattern sabres with scabbard was 1090 mm.

Holsters and Bandoliers

A lot of the personal equipment used by the Italian army was of pre-World War I vintage and although efforts were being made to update the equipment used, the process was slow. Even by the beginning of World War II much of this obsolete equipment was still in widespread use, and so the Italian soldier went to war with equipment little changed from that worn in World War I.

The holster for the model 1889 Glisenti revolver came in several colours and materials – grey-green or khaki canvas, chemically dyed grey-green or brown leather, with pouch flaps secured by either a strap or a

Artillerymen wear the M91 bandolier for mounted soldiers. North Africa. (Otto Meyer)

Infantry soldiers wear the M1907 grey/green leather ammunition pouches for the Carcano rifle and carbine. 29 January, 1940. Maselica, Italy. (Sergio Andreanelli)

metal stud. Some had two leather straps on the rear for affixing to a bandolier while others had a belt loop.

There were numerous types of leather holsters for the Beretta Model 34, some with a spare magazine pouch on the outside, others without; front pouch flaps that covered the whole or part of the holster were secured either by straps or by metal press studs. A variety of coloured leather was used – grey-green, brown and black. Some models had back straps or clips which enabled them to be attached to a bandolier instead of a belt.

The holster for the Model 1910 Glisenti was made of grey-green leather with an external magazine pouch. The pistol was held by a flap secured by a leather strap threaded through a metal clip. The holster was initially adopted by cavalry officers during World War I and could be worn with a bandolier attached to a ring fixed at the inner upper left corner of the holster.

Two basic patterns of grey-green leather bandolier of pre-World War I vintage were widely used by cavalry, armoured, artillery and transport personnel. The first was a three-pouch bandolier known as the

Model 1874/1889 which carried pistol ammunition for the 1889 revolver. A slightly different pouch interior was available for carrying a clip of ammunition in each, for the Model 1934 Beretta. The pistol holster was hung from a metal terminal ring at the base of the bandolier.

The second type had two pouches and was known as the Model 1891; it held ammunition for the Carcano rifle or carbine. At the base on some a small leather pouch was attached to carry two spare clips of rifle ammunition. Pistol and revolver holsters could also be worn on this bandolier. A brown leather version of the two-pouch bandolier was worn by colonial soldiers and some members of the Blackshirt Militias.

A number of variations of the brown leather bandolier were used by the Fascist Militia. Two- and three-pouch types could be of varying shapes and sizes – some carried rifle ammunition, others pistol rounds. Pistol holsters were often attached to the terminal rings at the bottom. These bandoliers were of makeshift manufacture and were never officially recognised by either the army or the MVSN.

The rig most widely issued to infantry was again of pre-World War I vintage and was worn up to and during World War II. This was a combination which included an M1891 grey-green leather waist belt secured by an open metal-frame buckle, with two M1907 leather cartridge-pouches worn at the front of the belt, which was threaded through two loops on the rear. A leather suspender strap which clipped on to a rear loop between the two pouches was put around the neck and attached again to the loop. By this unusual arrangement the belt and pouches were supported, though this placed undue strain on the wearer's neck. It was also uncomfortable when the soldier was required to lie on his stomach. A brown leather version was issued to colonial soldiers.

A variation of the grey-green double pouch was used, but it had no metal loop on the rear and was worn on the belt without the neck suspender, a much more comfortable combination.

A similar rig was issued to Alpini ski soldiers, though in white canvas. It had four pouches that were an integral part of a wide belt which split into two smaller straps at the rear secured by a hook-and-clip arrangement. The neck suspender strap hooked on to the pouches as the leather rig did.

Canvas and leather pouches similar in appearance to the German MP38/40 type were issued for carrying three magazines of the M38 MAB. The front flaps were secured by short leather belts which clipped on to metal studs.

The rear of the pouch was reinforced with leather and had two loops for wearing on a belt at an angle, and a metal clip for connecting to a leather suspender strap that was worn around the neck and secured to another pouch on the belt in an arrangement similar to the 1907 infantry rig.

A grey-green or khaki canvas carrying-bag was used by paratroops for holding the M38 MAB during combat jumps. The bag had a flap at the top which was strapped closed – when opened it revealed a large pouch for holding the M38. A variable number of pouches for holding ammunition magazines, tools and cord were fastened on the outside. A long canvas strap ran the length of the bag, secured at each end by metal lugs, for wearing over the shoulder when on the ground.

A novel method for carrying the M38 bag during a jump was employed by the Italians. A pouch was secured to the paratroopers left ankle, and the muzzle of the gun-bag fitted into it; the butt was secured to the wearer's thigh and attached to a five-metre length of coiled rope. After the soldier had jumped from the plane and his parachute had opened, the bag would be removed from the ankle pouch and the rope uncoiled so it could dangle below him as he descended. When he landed the bag was retrieved and the paratrooper was ready for action.

The Breda M30 6.5 mm had a grey-green leather or khaki webbing pouch containing stripping and cleaning tools which was worn on the belt by one of the machine-gun crew.

The officers' pattern belt was very similar to the British Sam Browne belt, but differed in that it had a false open frame brass buckle through which the belt was threaded and fastened on to the left side by a brass stud. A leather strap was worn over the right shoulder, while the pistol holster was worn on the wearer's left. However, if a dagger was worn it was placed on the left and the holster moved to the right. (In fact Italian officers did also wear the British pattern, which was of sturdier construction than the Italian model.)

Knapsacks, Rucksacks and Haversacks

All packs issued to Italian military personnel were made of a light, waterproof canvas which came in a variety of colours – stone grey, grey-green or khaki. Straps were of grey-green webbing or leather.

The Model 1939 was a small, general-purpose knapsack, with the front flap secured by two vertical leather straps fastened by metal studs. At the rear were two webbing straps with spring clips and D rings which enabled the haversack to be worn either on the back or over the shoulder. On the top centre of the haversack, on each side at the bottom corners and underneath in two locations were straps and metal buckles to which any two of the following could be strapped: a rolled greatcoat, camouflage shelter-quarter or a blanket, depending on preference. Inside were three evenly divided pockets, the centre one having a flap which was secured shut by a leather strap. Some variations of this pack were made, though the basic layout remained much the same.

A large webbing rucksack, similar in appearance to the World War II German rucksack, was issued to Alpini troops in 1939 and also used by the MVSN. It comprised a big central pouch closed at the top by a drawstring with a smaller full-length pocket flanking it

Italian POWs captured in North Africa 1942 carry a variety of personal equipment such as water bottles, gas-mask bags and haversacks. (ATL, Wellington, New Zealand)

on either side. All three pouches were covered by small flaps with webbing belts. There was a webbing strap for fastening equipment to the top centre of the haversack, two on each side and two on the bottom. On the back were two vertical carrying straps, also made of webbing.

A heavy drill cotton haversack called a tactical bag, similar to the German World War II bread bag, was used by troops in the front line. It had a quarter-length flap which was fastened by two green plastic buttons. A small pouch on the top edge of the pack was used to hold field bandages. A webbing shoulder strap was attached at the top corners of the bag, in which were normally carried essentials such as a mess tin, food, hand grenades and rifle ammunition.

A soft grey canvas pouch measuring 26 cm by 39 cm with a front flap and two cloth straps for tying was used to carry spare clothing such as a shirt, socks and underwear.

Gas-Masks

The model 1933 gas-mask was contained in a square bag with a three-quarter flap front and webbing shoulder strap. The inside was divided into two segments, one to house the mask-piece, the other for the filter cylinder. On the top outside edge, covered by the flap, was a cloth pocket which contained a spare rubber inlet/outlet valve and spare lenses.

The face-mask was of grey or brown moulded rubber with two eye-pieces of clear, splinterless glass, with webbing-covered elastic straps at the top for securing on to the head. At the base of the mask was a valve holder connected to a length of corrugated rubber hosing, which was in turn joined to a cylindrical filter. This gas-mask afforded adequate protection against most common types of warfare gases.

The Type 35 gas-mask was contained in a cylindrical bag with a flap front and a webbing shoulder strap. Inside was a single compartment which contained the mask-piece and filter cylinder, plus a metal container with a spare rubber inlet valve. The face-mask was much the same as the Model 33, though the outlet valve was opposite the mouth and the inlet valve was contained in a short metal screw adaptor into which the cylinder filter canister was screwed, dispensing with the long rubber hose.

Water Bottles and Mess Tins

The standard-issue water bottle for infantry and cavalry was the Model 1933, of one-litre capacity, constructed of aluminium with a rounded shoulder, and covered with grey-green or khaki wool (dampening the wool was meant to keep the contents cool). A webbing strap for wearing over the shoulder was attached on the upper edges by aluminium lugs. The screw-top plug had a small mouthpiece with a removable valve which enabled water to be sipped to help economise on water consumption in the field. A bottle with the same features – though with a larger (two-litre) capacity – was also used by Alpini and the Fascist Militia.

Another aluminium bottle, more rounded than the former types and of one-litre capacity, was issued to infantry in Ethiopia. Covered with grey-green wool, it had a short webbing strap that ran from the back to the front, with a leather extension that attached to a metal stud. This arrangement was worn on the waist belt. The screw-top plug did not have a valve at the top.

A variation of this bottle had the short leather and webbing strap removed and a longer webbing strap (for wearing over shoulder) re-threaded through three leather lugs sewn around the outer edges of the wool cover.

An aluminium kidney-shaped cylinder 40 cm high with a 6.25-litre capacity was used as a bulk water container. This had a wire carrying handle attached to the upper edges; on the top to one side was a large screw-top plug for filling. On top of that was a smaller, threaded plug for pouring water out.

An olive green or dark khaki (for Africa) painted aluminium mess tin was part of all equipment. Of semi-circular two-piece construction, the bottom half consisted of a deep pot with a wire carrying handle, and a cover with a smaller handle which could also be used as a dish.

A small kidney-shaped aluminium cup with a folding handle was carried inside the larger mess tin.

A grey linen cover with a loop on the rear for a leather securing strap to pass through was used to hold the mess tin when not in use.

An aluminium spoon and fork were standard-issue eating utensils. These had the royal coat of arms stamped on the handles with the initials R(egio) E(sercito) – Royal Army.

A small, square, fold-out dish warmer made of pressed tin was also issued. This was heated by pieces of solid fuel supplied in segments of ten to a packet with the warmer.

Shelter-Quarters

The Model 1929 camouflage shelter-quarter was made of tightly woven waterproof cotton drill. The European issue version was a patch pattern of forest green, chestnut brown and light grey-green. A khaki version was made for use in Africa, though the European style was used there as well.

Issued to each soldier along with the shelter-quarter were two or three metal tent-pole segments, each 41 cm long, and 30.5 cm long metal pegs. These enabled shelter quarters to be joined with a variable number of other shelters to construct tents of various shapes and sizes holding up to twenty soldiers.

Shelter-quarters could also be worn as ponchos or used as ground sheets or bedding covers. They were popular with Allied soldiers when they could obtain them as ground sheets and tents. The Germans seized large stocks of the camouflage M29 material in Italy in 1943 and manufactured a variety of camouflage uniform items for issue to German soldiers in Italy.

Miscellaneous

All troops were required to carry at least one field dressing in their kit. This was wrapped in waterproof paper and had a string tab to enable easy opening.

Alpini troops had two specialist items issued. The first was a ice axe with a steel pick-head, a long wooden shaft with a sliding metal ring attached to a canvas wrist strap and a metal spike at the base. The second was the M1934 walking stick – a rounded length of wood 146 cm long which had a blunt metal cap at the top with a leather wrist strap attached and a small metal spike at the base.

Officer Accoutrements

The binoculars used by army officers were of a 6 × 30 or 8 × 30 prismatic type, bought privately but of officially approved styles. Artillery officers had their lenses with grid radians. All glasses were black with brown leatherette grips and had a leather strap for wearing around the neck.

The carrying case was of brown or green leather and had a long leather strap for wearing over the shoulder or a loop for wearing on the waist belt.

Compasses used by officers were of various designs of approved military standards, and were carried in a leather pouch worn on the waist belt.

The regulation officers' map case was of brown leather and had a half-flap secured by two clip studs to the front of the case; when unfolded, this revealed a two-segment leather frame with a clear celluloid grid behind which maps could be placed. Behind one of the grids was a deep pocket for storage of such items as pens, pencils, paper, etc. Numerous unofficial map cases were also used by officers.

Model 1929 shelter-quarters made up into a tent. This particular one has sustained some damage from shell splinters. Tobruk front, North Africa, 1941. (Author's collection)

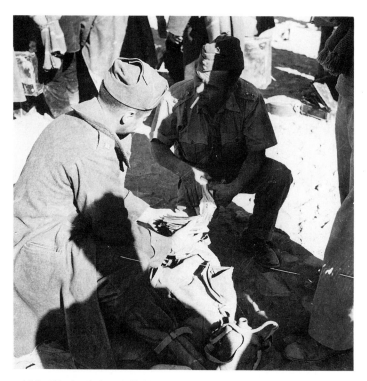

A New Zealand Army officer examines the papers of an Italian
captured in Egypt during the first Libyan campaign in 1941.
(ATL, Wellington, New Zealand)

Chapter Six
Documents and Insignia

Evaluation Book

THE FASCIST cradle-to-grave philosophy of regimenting its citizens throughout their life applied particularly to their paramilitary and military activities, where the citizen's progress through the military indoctrination process was documented in a series of booklets known generally as the *libretto personale* or evaluation book. All male citizens from the ages of eleven to thirty-two were required to keep this book. In addition to information on the physical health of the owner, it contained an evaluation of his intellectual, sporting, social, political and military activities.

The book was divided into five chapters, each devoted to a different phase of the citizen soldier's military career. The first was on the Balilla; next the Vanguard; then Young Fascists; military service and, finally, post-military service. The book was retained and presented to authorities when required.

Individual Record Book

This book was issued to other ranks and NCOs on commencement of military service; it was meant to cover the whole of the soldier's military career and did not serve as a pay book. The front cover recorded the name, number, regiment and company or equivalent level (the last two by rubber stamp).

The information covered a variety of details on the personal and military background of the bearer: parents' names; place and date of birth; religion; place of residence; military district; marital status; civil occupation and academic qualifications; physical description serving as a means of checking identity; record of vaccinations for smallpox, typhus, etc; record of any hospitalisation; details of call-up, transfers and units served in; any specialities, such as ability to drive, or ride horses, foreign languages spoken, skill as a wood-worker, etc; proficiency in target shooting; list of weapons issued, with serial numbers, and comprehensive record of all clothing and equipment.

The following list is reproduced from the individual record book of an 'other rank' of the 8 Compagnia, 63 Reggimento Fanteria, Divisione Cagliari, issued in 1931 to Fedrico Ruffiuatti, who lived in the military district of Turin, northern Italy.

Item	Number issued
Collar badge	2
Towels	2
Field cap	1
Field cap rigid form	1
Water bottle	1
Cleaning kit in bag	1
Cotton socks	3 pairs
Cotton shirts	3 pairs
Belt for trousers	1
Ties woollen or linen	3
Spoon	1
Doublet	1

Body belt	2
Puttees	2 pairs
Handkerchief	3
Metal badges for epaulettes	1 pair
Metal badge for fatigue cap	1
Mess tin	1
Woollen fatigue jacket	1
Parade jacket	1
Linen jacket	2
Gloves	1 pair
Long underpants	1 pair
Short underpants	1 pair
Small cape	1
Woollen fatigue trousers	1 pair
Parade trousers	1 pair
Linen – long trousers	1 pair
Linen – short trousers	1 pair
Pair of tent poles	
Dog tag	1
Small bag for hard tack	1
Small bag for used clothing	1
Shoe-polish boxes	
Hair brush	1
Shoe brush	1
Boots	2 pairs
Metal stars	3 pairs
Haversack	1
Camo quarter-shelter	1
Small haversack	1
Plimsolls	1 pair
PE shorts	1 pair
Identification card	1

MVSN Identification Booklet

All members of the MVSN were required to carry an identification card the size of a small pocket book. On the inside of the front cover was the owner's photograph and a specimen signature in ink. On the first page was recorded the owner's name, parents' names, place and date of birth, rank, military serial number, legion headquarters stamp and the commander's signature in ink.

There was a four-segment fold-out on which were recorded campaigns in which the bearer had served, decorations received, wounds, date of enlistment and promotions.

A card insert was carried with the ID card. This was printed on one side and had a physical description of the bearer, unit, place and date of birth, signature in ink, military number, rubber stamp of legion and commander's signature in ink.

Warrant Officer and Officer Pay Book

This was almost exclusively a pay book and was renewed every year. Inside were recorded sundry details such as unit (shown by a rubber stamp) name, place and date of birth, military district, rank, marital status and date of issue.

Other pages dealt with the recording of various emoluments paid to the bearer.

Military Pay

The army's Administrative Service was responsible for paying the military. Other ranks and NCOs' records of pay were kept by the service. Officers and warrant officers were paid every month, while in the Royal Army other ranks and NCOs up to the rank of sergeant-major received their pay every ten days: this was known as decade pay. Fascist Militia other ranks and NCOs were paid monthly.

The 1943 exchange rate was approximately nineteen lire to the US dollar. Monthly rates of pay for the Royal Army by rank, with maximum allowance, in 1943 US$ were:

Officers	
Marshal of Italy	316.83
General of army	244.33
General of army corps	215.16
Divisional general	190.16
Brigade general	154.50
Colonel	122.58
Lieutenant-Colonel	113.25
Major	96.59
Captain	87.50
Lieutenant	73.00
Second Lieutenant	58.25
Warrant Officer	27.99 to 29.51

Other ranks and NCOs	
Sergeant-Major	18.99 to 25.71
Corporal	1.85 to 2.21
Private	1.51

Married men received an extra allowance of $12.80 a month, plus $4.80 for each child. During World War II many officers, NCOs and other ranks received a 75 per cent increase in pay. Called a War Allowance, it was paid to those who served at the front. The families of soldiers lost in battle received pensions rated according to the deceased's former rank, years of service and decorations.

Blackshirt Antonio D'Angelo recalls an incident while stationed in Libya:

I remember that my mother was paid 28c [100 centesimi = 1 lire] a day, which was Royal Army pay, and which by some error went on for months. Mothers of volunteer Blackshirts, especially the sons of a widowed mother (as I was), were supposed to get 5 lire a day. After my mother wrote to me about this several times, I tried to get the officer in my unit to straighten it out, but he put me off.

I went absent without leave to get to see Marshal Graziani, who was at a command post. I was arrested at first, but when I finally was able to explain my mother's situation to Graziani, he released me from confinement and all the officers in my legion were fined from their monthly pay until all my mother's back payments were taken care of.

Most of the Blackshirts in the 28th Ottobre were already veterans of Ethiopian and Spanish wars and a certain amount of respect was granted to them by greener soldiers, especially those who had been awarded the Cross of Valour or Merit Cross (as I had). Marshal Graziani had a special admiration for veterans of earlier campaigns.

Military Postal Service

The Military Postal Service was responsible for the distribution and collection of all official and private correspondence, for savings bank and money postal services, and for the dispatch and receipt of all private telegrams for the field army. During World War II the Military Postal Service operated in Italy, Albania, France, Corsica, Greece, Crete, Yugoslavia, Libya, Egypt, Tunisia, Poland, Romania, Russia, Hungary, the Aegean Islands and East Africa.

Each army, army corps and division was allocated a military post number, which in the majority of cases was used by that formation throughout its existence. All that was required was the recipient's name, rank and the military post number (although information down to company or battery level was often included by the sender) for the mail to be directed to the soldier in any particular formation.

The service was to all practical purposes discontinued on Armistice Day, 8 September 1943, although fragmented offices did continue to function – though without co-ordination – after this date.

Ranks

In the Royal Army and Fascist Militia, commissioned ranks were divided into three groups: general officers, superior officers, and junior officers. Above the rank of general there were two Marshals of the Empire, the king and Mussolini. In addition there were six Marshals of Italy.

There are a few peculiarities in the Italian system not readily shown by means of a chart. For instance, the ranks of lieutenant-general and major-general, equivalent to US major-general and brigadier-general respectively were reserved for the artillery, engineer and other branches. The title of first captain or first lieutenant were given to any captain or first lieutenant who had held his respective rank for twelve years. Army head chaplains had the rank of captain. Band leaders and fencing masters were second lieutenants.

The corporal in the Italian army is not an NCO, but is equated with the US private First Class.

Certain ranks of officers and NCOs in the Fascist Militia were known by the Italian version of the ancient Roman titles.

Collar Patches and Devices

All infantry regiments of the line wore coloured collar patches on either side of the tunic collar just above the lapel. All arms and services were distinguished by a specific colour. Collar patches and devices were often absent on tropical uniform.

Plain or striped rectangles when used alone denoted divisional infantry. When they carried a flame or other superimposed device they indicated the divisional unit of the arm or service it characterised.

Braids were worn on a coloured background by the Royal Carabinieri, the Grenadiers and the general staff. The Grenadier patches had precisely the same significance as the infantry rectangles, and were also used in combination with other devices.

Single flames denoted artillery, engineers, various services, the Frontier Guard or garrison troops, and were either in plain colours or in black or green with a coloured background or coloured piping. They were superimposed on either rectangles or braid. Two pointed flames were worn by Alpini, Bersaglieri, tank units, Motor Transport Corps, Finance Guards and the Fascist Militia. Three pointed flames were worn only by the cavalry.

A reserve second lieutenant of the army postal service. The single pointed flames on his collars are thought to be orange.

Captain Giovanino Laterza of the Giovani Fascisti regiment wears the sahariana with stars but no flames. (Franco Festa)

Second lieutenant Giuseppe Fassio of a Bersaglieri motorcycle machine-gun battalion wears the double crimson flame of the Bersaglieri with the red and white striped rectangle for machine-gunners superimposed over it.

This captain of the VIII sector of the frontier guard has a green tunic collar with red piping for GAF infantry. The sector badges were always numbered with Roman numerals.

A second lieutenant of 53 regiment, Umberia infantry division, wears his greatcoat with stars but no flames on the collars.

A captain of the 141 legion wears the double black flames with fascio of the Fascist Militia.

A private of the bridging engineers with the single black flame with violet piping, which was worn by all branches of the engineer corps.

Three artillerymen of the 80 artillery regiment, La Spezia division, displaying the black single flame with yellow piping of the artillery corps.

A transport corps major wears the black double flames on blue square collar insignia. Note the austere modified wartime cordellino uniform for officers, which is in stark contrast to the bullion weave bustina insignia. (Author's collection)

Gallantry Medals

Great emphasis and importance was placed upon gallantry awards in the Italian armed forces. Military sentinels were required to salute people in civilian clothes who had been decorated for valour or for wounds received in action, as well as mothers and widows wearing decorations of dead soldiers. Officers and other ranks who had not been decorated for valour or distinction in war were to salute those men of the same grade who had these distinctions.

As a general rule medals were not actually awarded but, as in several other European countries (France and Belgium for example), most were required to be purchased by the recipient. This led to great diversification among competing manufacturers who varied the authorised ribbon colours and made a bronze-coloured award also in silver because it looked better, or vice versa. In many cases recipients did not follow the rules and regulations as to the proper order of the decorations and added all manner of unauthorised bars, stars, etc.

Grenadier corporals display their distinctive corps collar insignia. Rome, May 1941. (Author's collection)

Mussolini awards a Gold Medal for Military Valour to a Young Fascist. Rome, 30 May 1942. (Museum Rgt. Vol. GGFF, Ponti sul Mincio, Italy)

The highest award for military gallantry in action, if not by precedence certainly by the esteem it bestowed, was called the Military Valour Medal. It came in two grades, gold and silver, and was instituted on 26 March 1833, by King Carlo Alberto. A bronze award was added in 1887.

The circular medal was the same design for all three grades in the army (the navy and air force had their own designs). The obverse of the army medal bore the arms of Savoy and a wreath with an oak and laurel sprig surmounted by a crown and surrounded by the words AL VALORE MILITARE. On the reverse was a laurel wreath, between which the recipient's name and unit were engraved. The place and date of the action were engraved in the space between the upper part of the wreath and the edge of the medal.

Granted to all ranks, the Military Valour Medal could be earned several times by the same individual. The ribbon for all three grades was a bright blue moiré (the colour of the Royal House of Savoy).

A variation was awarded to native soldiers. On the obverse, instead of the Savoy arms, was a portrait of the king.

Holders of the decoration or their families received an annual pension. The gold medal (at 1943 exchange rates) was worth US $75, the silver $38 and the bronze $15.

A lesser grade award instituted by royal decree in January 1918, had a bronze Greek cross with the words MERITO DI GUERRA on the obverse, surmounted by the royal monogram and the crown on the upper limb, and an upraised sword and oak leaves on the bottom limb. On the reverse was a central star with the rays reaching the edges.

This medal was awarded for being mentioned in dispatches, serving on the front line for a long period of time, being wounded in battle or for gallantry in action.

There was no limit to the number of awards, as any addition was indicated by a crown worn on the ribbon: bronze for three to four, silver for five to seven and gold for eight to ten. However, in most cases the recipients of multiple crosses wore each individual award rather than the crowns on a single medal.

An infantry officer is decorated by his commanding officer.
(Author's collection)

In January 1922 the cross was changed to make it a junior award to the Military Valour Medal, to be awarded only in wartime, and only for valour. A bronze sword was added to the ribbon to distinguish this award from the 1918 cross.

In October 1941 a new cross much the same as the previous version was introduced, with the same colour of ribbon and a bronze sword. This was supposed to be inscribed CROCE AL VALORE MILITARE, but in practice only VALORE MILITARE was usually inscribed. The cross was awarded for military valour during peacetime. The same blue and white ribbon was used. In September 1942 the inscription was changed by statute to read AL VALORE MILITARE, but this again seems to have been ignored by manufacturers, as the cross still read VALORE MILITARE. In May 1943 the blue and white cross ribbon was changed to the blue worn on the Military Valour Medal.

Order of Precedence for Wearing Medals

When medals were worn for full dress or the ribbons for service or field wear there was a prescribed order of precedence. The highest grade medals or ribbons were on the wearer's right, down to lesser grade on the left.

The military Valour Medal as illustrated in the 1910 regulations. All three grades – bronze, silver and gold – were of the same design. The rear of the medal was inscribed with the recipient's name, date and location of the action for which the medal was awarded.

A beribboned Italian priest captured in Tunisia, North Africa, is given a mug of water by a New Zealand soldier. Note the large cross on his tunic pocket – it was red and worn by military chaplains only. (ATL, Wellington, New Zealand)

The order of precedence was:

Supreme Order of Our Lady of the Annunciation
The Military Orders of Savoy
Gold, Silver and Bronze Medal of Military Valour
War Cross of Military Valour
Orders of the Saints Maurice and Lazarus
The Civil Order of Savoy
Mauritian Medal for Fifty Years in Military Service
Gold, Silver and Bronze Civil Valour Medal
Wars of Independence Medal
Decorations of the Order of the Crown of Italy
Merit Medal for Public Health
Medal for Campaign in Eritrea
Cross for Seniority in Royal Army
Cross for Seniority for Finance Guard
Order of Merit of Work
Medal for International Expedition to China
Long Command Medal for Officers and NCOs of the Royal
 Army and Finance Guard
Medal for Italian-Turkish Campaign in Libya 1911–12
Order of the Colonial Star of Italy
Medal of Merit for Public Sanitation
War Merit Cross
Medal commemorating 1915–18 War
United Italy Medal
Fiume Expedition Commemorative Medal

Commemorative Medal for Italian East Africa Operations
Medal for Volunteers in 1915-18 War
Medal for Volunteers in East Africa
Medal for Military Operations in Spain
Medal for Volunteers in Spain
Medal for March on Rome
Cross for Service in the MVSN
Red Cross Merit Medal

Identity Discs

The identity disc worn around the neck of all soldiers could be found in two variations. The one used extensively during World War II was of light metal two-piece construction which could be split into two identical plates, one of which was kept with the body, the other sent home with the deceased's personal effects.

All the details on the plate were stamped in relief. A breakdown of a typical identity disc of this type is shown here:

12329 – Serial number
(102) – Code number of military district
C – Catholic
Rosati – Surname
Fedro – Christian name
Di Cesare E Di – Father's Christian name
Taddei – Mother's maiden name
Maria – Mother's Christian name
CL.1921 – Year of birth, i.e. conscript class
Com. S. Croce – Hometown
Pisa – Province

The format changed every few years, but the basic information was always the same.

Another type which was used during World Wars I and II was a small square metal locket in which was contained a strip of paper which folded out and had recorded on it basic information about the wearer – such as Christian name and surname, year of birth, military district, birthplace, names of mother and father, where mobilised and unit assigned to. On the reverse was details of medical inoculations.

Arm Shields

The first official sleeve shield of the Royal Army was introduced in September 1934. The sleeve shield regulation called for its use by officers, NCOs and other ranks in all commands of the Royal Army. The shield was applied to the left sleeve, 15 cm from the shoulder, above the other insignia of rank or speciality. It could also have been worn by reservists as a remembrance of the unit in which they had served.

The first shields adopted by the army were solid brass with dark blue enamel for all officers and Warrant officers; brass stamping of the identical shield for NCOs and other ranks. All shields had a tiny hole at each corner so they could be sewn on to the tunic sleeve. Officers' shields carried the stamping of Lorioli & Castelli, Milano, the firm that made the majority of shields. Other ranks' shields were painted a darker blue than the enamel of officers' shields: one was occasionally encountered with an almost blue-black paint. There were two types of the other ranks' pattern: one had a wider border, similar to a double-step around the shield. Other variations were in the size of the number and letters, and in the print of the letters and numbers.

The Alpini divisions used an identically shaped shield, but with green enamel for officers and green paint for NCOs and other ranks. Uniquely in the Alpini there was a special shield for Superior Alpini Command for officers and other ranks belonging to Command Staff.

In 1935, a red shield of the same design and size was officially adopted for motorised divisions. Additionally, it was stamped with the newly-formed Divisione Motorizzata title. A red shield was also allotted to the four infantry divisions permanently stationed in Libya.

In 1935 seven army divisions of the Royal Army were mobilised for the Ethiopian War. As these were sent to Africa, new divisions of the same name were raised in Italy at each one's home station. The number one hundred was added to the division's original number and II to the name to distinguish it from the same division overseas.

In 1938, the metal sleeve shields were substituted with cloth shields. Infantry officers and warrant officers wore gold bullion on blue felt; NCOs and other ranks had a machine-loom-woven version made of rayon. Here, the design was confined within a large shield-shaped patch with a straight top. The shields were embroidered in yellow thread on the colours of the specific branch – blue for infantry, red for motorised and green for Alpini.

Cavalry divisions wore a blue shield – the same as the infantry – stamped Divisione Celere on the left.

In 1937, a special shield was adopted by the Frontier Guard and since these came into being after the metal shield was abolished, they are only found in gold

A portrait study of officers from a variety of corps displaying rank insignia on sleeves and shoulder boards, some with arm shields.
(Author's collection)

bullion on green felt for officers and machine-loom woven on green for other ranks.

They were worn also by the infantry, artillery and engineers assigned to the guard. They were easily distinguished from infantry and Alpini shields as a band was designed across an upraised Roman short sword, with the number of the guard sector shown in Roman numerals, and the standard oak leaves. Artillery officers had a bright orange band in the centre of the shield matching the colour of its piping.

In the same year, two additional shields were adopted by soldiers assigned to the Italian territories of Zara and Elba. These were white with blue lettering for Truppe di Zara and all blue with white lettering for Truppe dell' Elba. Again, these came in only fabric – bullion and embroidery for officers and machine-loom woven for NCOs and other ranks.

By the end of 1938, all infantry divisions in Italy were being reorganised and many divisional names and numbers were changed, which is why some shields do not correspond with the post-1940 World War II field division.

Lack of strict enforcement of regulations yielded a variety of shields well into World War II, though technically they should have been off the uniform by 1940.

The Divisione Paracadutisti Folgore or Nembo never had sleeve shields. Paratroops did not exist as a fighting unit in 1934 – when metal shields were adopted – or in 1938, when the cloth ones came into use. These divisions were organised after 1940, by which time sleeve shields had already been abolished.

Italian divisions were named after various subjects, including such cities as Forli, Torino or Trento, or rivers such as Rubicone, Po or Isonzo. Others adopted names of mountains like Gran Sasso or Monte Nero. Some commemorated the Royal House of Savoy: among these were Savoia, Sabauda and Superga, where initially the kingdom of Sardinia was based in Turin. Cavalry divisions, long the élite of the monarchy, were all named after members of the House of Savoy – dukes, princes and kings. The infantry divisions permanently stationed in Libya were named after ancient Libyan cities and towns.

The Royal Army Division names and numbers used on shields were:

Cavalry or Rapid Divisions
1st Eugenio di Savoia
2nd Emanuele Filiberto Testa di Ferro
3rd Principe Amedeo Duca d'Aosta

Alpini Divisions – Mountain Infantry and Artillery
1st Taurinense
2nd Tridentina
3rd Julia
4th Guneense
5th Pusteria

Motorised Divisions
1st Trento
8th Po
101st Trieste

Metropolitan Infantry Divisions in Libya
60th Sabrata
61st Sirte
62nd Marmarica*
63rd Cirene

*The Marmarica was also found with a star in place of the 62 and it was worn by Libyan (native or coloured) soldiers.

Colonial Infantry Divisions
Two divisions of askari (native) soldiers were raised and placed under Italian command in the colonies. Their shields have only been found in blue machine-loom weave with yellow letters and with the star in place of the number. They are:

Divisione Libia
Divisione Eritrea

Infantry Divisions
1st Superga
2nd Sforzesca
3rd Monferrato
4th Monviso
5th Cosseria
6th Legnano
7th Leonessa
8th Po*
9th Pasubio
10th Piave
11th Brennero
12th Timavo
13th Monte Nero
14th Isonzo
15th Carnaro
16th Fossalta
17th Rubicone
18th Metauro
19th Gavinana
20th Curtatone e Montanara
21st Grantiere di Sardegna
22nd Cacciatori delle Alpi

23rd Murge
24th Gran Sasso
25th Volturno
26th Assietta
27th Sila
28th Vespri
29th Peloritana
30th Sabauda
31st Caprera

Additionally, sleeve shields were manufactured for some divisions after 1937 and found only in fabric:

36th Forli
52nd Torino
7th Lupi di Toscana

*8th PO is not to be confused with the Motorised.

Territorial Soldiers
Found only in fabric

Truppe di Zara – no numbers – stationed in Zara
Truppe dell' Elba – no numbers – stationed on the Island of Elba
Granatieri di Savoia – no numbers – stationed in Italian East Africa

Divisions Reorganised as Secondary Division Stationed in Italy
105th Cosseria II
119th Gavinana II
124th Gran Sasso II
126th Assietta II
127th Sila II
129th Peloritana II
130th Sabauda II

Fascist Militia Zone Shields

Italy was divided into fifteen recruitment zones for the MVSN of which fourteen zones had shields. All had different colours and numerals. No shield was ever designed for the fifteenth zone, the island of Sardinia.

Shields were basically the same – Roman eagle in a circle at the top portion of the shield, the word ZONA on the left, and CCNN on the right. Roman numerals were at the bottom. In the centre there was one of five emblems:

1. A *fascio* for Headquarters
2. An upraised Roman short sword for assault troops
3. Crossed rifles for riflemen
4. A flaming bomb for grenadiers
5. A machine-gun for machine-gunners

The shields were brass for other ranks and NCOs and gold-weave bullion for officers.

Following are the sections of Italy where each zone was headquartered and the colours of each of those zones.

I Zona – Piedmont area, headquartered in Turin – top green, bottom amaranth
II Zona – Lombardy area, headquartered in Milan – top green, bottom blue
III Zona – Liguria area, headquartered in Genoa – top green, bottom red
IV Zona – Venezia-Tridentina area, headquartered in Verona – all blue
V Zona – Veneto area, headquartered in Venice – top green, bottom silver
VI Zona – Venezia-Giulia area, headquartered in Trieste – top green, bottom black
VII Zona – Emilia-Romagna area, headquartered in Bologna – all amaranth
VIII Zona – Tuscany area, headquartered in Florence – all silver
IX Zona – Umbria-Marche area, headquartered in Perugia – all red
X Zona – Lazio region, headquartered in Rome – all black
XI Zona – Abbruzzi-Molise area, headquartered in Pescara – top blue, bottom red
XII Zona – Campania area, headquartered in Naples – top blue, bottom black
XIII Zona – Puglie area, headquartered in Bari – top red, bottom black
XIV Zona – Sicily, headquartered in Palermo – top silver, bottom red

Militia Shields

In 1935 seven Blackshirt divisions were raised for the Ethiopian campaign and an arm shield was designated for each one. The design was a Roman-style eagle with outstretched wings in a wreath at the top, sitting on a *fascio*, with the divisional number at the bottom and the name around the sides.

For other ranks the shield was stamped brass or aluminium with black paint or black woven synthetic thread with white highlights. Black felt cloth with silver wire embroidery was for NCOs, and gold wire embroidery for officers. The Fascist Militia was in many ways a very individualistic organisation and as such its members did not always conform exactly to regulations: officers sometimes wore other-ranks quality shields and vice versa, the type often depending on availability and on how much money was on hand.

The seven CCNN divisions in Ethiopia were:

1 Divisione CCNN 23 Marzo
2 Divisione CCNN 28 Ottobre
3 Divisione CCNN 21 Aprile
4 Divisione CCNN 3 Gennaio
5 Divisione CCNN 1 Febbraio
6 Divisione CCNN Tevere
7 Divisione CCNN Cirene

General Headquarters personnel of the Blackshirt battalions in Rome had a black bakelite shield with a Roman eagle as a centrepiece clutching a sword in its talons; above the eagle were the initials MVSN and around the sides of the shield the words BTG. CC.NN. COMANDO GENERALE.

The four CCNN divisions raised for service in Libya had a new shield designed in 1938. This was similar to the earlier type worn in Ethiopia, except that the eagle had wings facing downwards within a circle, and instead of a *fascio* there was a Roman short sword facing upwards in the centre, with the division number at the bottom and its name around both sides. The word Libica was added to denote service in Libya.

The shields were made of stamped aluminium and were painted black with gilt highlights for all ranks. The four CCNN divisions in Libya were:

1 Divisione CCNN 23 Marzo Libica
2 Divisione CCNN 28 Ottobre Libica
3 Divisione CCNN 21 Aprile Libica
4 Divisione CCNN 3 Gennaio Libica

From 1939 the Albanian Militia had a round shield made of bakelite with a thin gold rim; a black double-headed eagle of Albania as a centrepiece with a gold *fascio* superimposed over it. The background was red. A version was also made in stamped silver metal, with a silver border and *fascio* on a black eagle with a red background. A bullion-embroidered version was manufactured for officers.

The Anti-Aircraft Militia's shield designed in 1938 had a Roman eagle at the top with the wings facing downwards, sitting on a horizontal *fascio* inside a circle at the top. At the bottom were the words MILIZIA CONTROAEREI and in the centre one of four designs: crossed cannons; crossed cannons with lightning bolts on either side; stylised wings with lightning bolts; a light AA machine-gun.

The shields for other ranks were made of light stamped aluminium painted black with gilded highlights. NCOs and officers had a black felt shield with gold wire embroidery.

The Coastal Defence Militia had a similar shield from 1938 with the initials MVSN near the top, above an anchor with the words ARTIGLIERIA MARIT-TIMA around the sides. This was made of stamped aluminium and painted blue, with gilded highlights.

From 1939 the combined headquarters of the Anti-Aircraft and Coastal Defence Militias wore a shield with the combination of the crossed cannons and an anchor as the centrepiece, with the words COM. MILIZIE. CONTROAEREI e ARTIG. MARIT-TIMA around the edges. It was made of heavy brass with red enamel for officers and stamped aluminium painted red for other ranks.

The Road Militia from 1938 had a shield with a *fascio* as the centrepiece with a stylised wing out the back, and a lion head on the top surmounted by the royal crown. The words MILIZIA NAZ. DELLA STRADA were around the sides. The shield was of stamped brass with blue painted background and gilt highlights for other ranks. A blue felt cloth and gold wire embroidered shield was for NCOs and officers; in addition officers could wear a brass and blue enamel pattern.

From 1938 the Frontier Militia also had a shield, with an eagle with downward-pointing wings within a circle at the top. In the centre was an ice pick-axe with a coil of rope in the shape of the Savoy knot intertwined around it; around the edges of the shield were the words MILIZIA DI FRONTIERA. The shield was made of stamped brass and had a painted green background with gilt highlights for other ranks. NCOs and officers had a green felt cloth version with wire embroidery or enamelled metal.

From 1938 also the Forestry Militia had a shield which showed an eagle with outstretched wings clutching a *fascio* in its talons. Underneath were crossed axes, with the words MILIZIA FORESTALE around the edges in silver highlight. The background was green. It was made of stamped brass with painted surface for other ranks and enamelled or embroidered for officers.

The University Militia version, also designed in 1938, featured at the top an eagle with outstretched wings sitting on a rifle and an open book. At the bottom point of the shield was a *fascio* with the words MILIZIA UNIVERSITARIA above. The highlights were in gilt while the background was white.

The shield was made of stamped brass with a painted surface for other ranks, while NCOs and officers had a shield of white felt with gold wire embroidery.

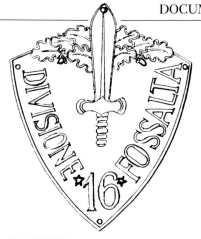

Illustration from military serial publication Number 54, circular 727 (1934) in which the new style of arm shield for infantry and Celere divisions is shown for the first time.

UFFICIALI E SOTTUFFICIALI   TRUPPA NAZIONALE   TRUPPA INDIGENA

Headwear badges worn by the Italian African Police as illustrated in their 1938 dress regulations. Officers and NCOs wore a gilt metal eagle with enamelled Savoy cross on the chest; the Italian other ranks had a bronze eagle with enameled cross while the native other ranks had a bronze eagle with no cross on the chest.

COCCARDA

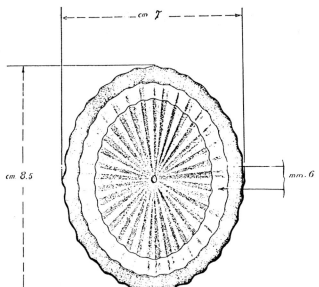

Cloth cockade also taken from an illustration in the 1938 Italian African Police regulations. This has roundels in the Italian national colours of red on outer rim, white in the middle and green in the centre. These were also worn by soldiers of all branches of the army as backing to headwear badges on the pith helmet in particular. The roundels were also found in several smaller sizes to the size illustrated.

In 1938 the Post and Telegraph Militia shield had a large *fascio* with a bugle superimposed over the centre, from which lightning bolts emerged. Over the top of the *fascio* was the royal crown, and around the bottom were the words MILIZIA POSTELEGRAFONICA. For other ranks the shield was brass with red paint. For officers it was gilt metal with red enamel.

The Port Militia also had a shield designed in 1938; it had an anchor over a horizontal *fascio* with the royal crown at the top as a centrepiece and the words MILIZIA PORTUARIA around the lower sides. Other ranks had a brass shield with red paint; for officers it was gilt metal with red enamel.

From July 1940 the wearing of arm shields was abolished for both the Royal Army and Fascist Militia for reasons of wartime security, but they were worn unofficially for some time after that.

Tav. LXXI

COMPLEMENTI DELL'UNIFORME

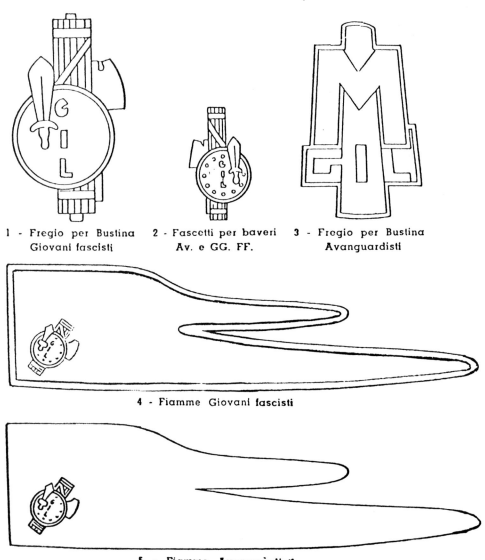

1 - Fregio per Bustina
Giovani fascisti

2 - Fascetti per baveri
Av. e GG. FF.

3 - Fregio per Bustina
Avanguardisti

4 - Fiamme Giovani fascisti

5 - Fiamme Avanguardisti

1942 dress regulations for the Fascist Youth showing the white metal cap badge for Young Fascist, the collar badge for Vanguards and Young Fascist, and the metal cap badge for Balilla and Vanguards. Collar flames for Young Fascists had a yellow border with red centre. The bottom flame for Vanguards is white.

DISTINTIVI DI GRADO

ORGANIZZATI

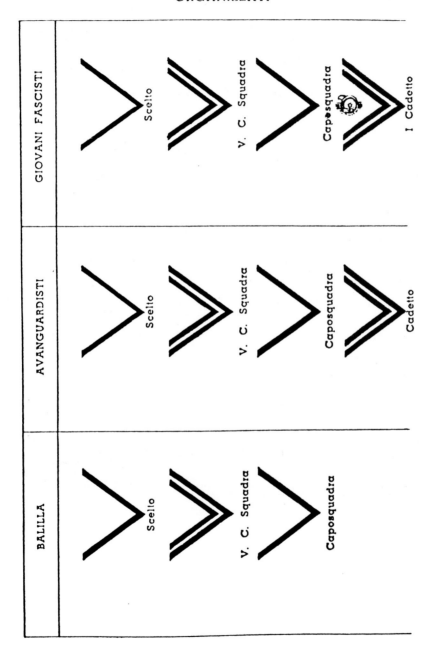

Rank table illustrated from the 1942 dress regulations for Fascist Youth. The top two rows of rank were in red while the bottom two were in yellow.

Signal

Un communiqué historique:

«Haut les mains!» ordonna à la garde de l'hôtel Otto Skorzeny, qui conduisit l'entreprise de libération du Duce. Désorientés et effrayés les carabinieri obéirent aussitôt.

La libération de Mussolini

Illustration taken from the German wartime propaganda magazine Signal illustrating the dramatic rescue of Benito Mussolini from the Hotel Campo Imperatore by a combined Luftwaffe and SS airborne force.

Chapter Seven
Armistice 1943,
The Beginning of the End

By THE TIME the armistice of 8 September 1943 was officially announced, Benito Mussolini had already received a vote of no-confidence from his own Fascist Grand Council headed by Dino Grandi. On the night of 24–25 July it voted by nineteen to eight to return all relevant powers and military conduct of the war to King Vittorio Emanuele III. On the afternoon of 25 July Mussolini was arrested after a visit to the king at Villa Savoia, where he had resigned as head of the government under pressure from the monarch.

He was spirited out of Rome and hidden in a number of secret locations in an attempt to thwart German efforts to locate him. Hitler had given orders that Mussolini be found and rescued as he wanted his old friend to establish a puppet Fascist government in German-occupied northern Italy.

Eventually located in the hotel Campo Imperatore in the Abruzzi Mountains in central Italy, he was rescued from his prison on 12 September during a daring glider raid by a combined Luftwaffe and SS assault group.

The Fascist government set up in German-held northern Italy was known as the Italian Social Republic – RSI – and comprised loyal followers of Mussolini and Fascism ready to fight to the death. Many were bitter over their betrayal by the army generals. The new Fascist army was known as the Republican National Guard (GNR), and comprised Blackshirt Militia members, along with units of the Carabinieri and the Italian Africa Police who had not surrendered with the Royal Army. What ensued in a divided Italy was in essence a civil war which ultimately led to the downfall of Fascism as a political power.

The king, his new Prime Minister Pietro Badoglio and their entourage, fled Rome early on the morning of 9 September, fearing for their own safety – a not unfounded concern as German Generalfeldmarschall Albrecht Kesselring that day moved in his soldiers to secure the capital and seal all exits. The group managed to escape the closing net and travel to Pescara on the Adriatic coast, then by the Italian naval corvette *Baionetta* to the southern port of Brindisi, which had only just been evacuated by the Germans.

The announcement of the armistice threw the Italian army into a state of bewilderment. The dilemma was compounded by the departure of the monarch and Badoglio at a time when the army was unclear how to react to moves by German or Allied forces.

The German divisions stationed in Italy saw the armistice as a betrayal and moved quickly to disarm the Italians in an operation codenamed 'ACHSE' (Axis), rendering them incapable of further effective resistance. Some soldiers did resist but found themselves grouped in isolated pockets where they were eventually subdued.

Caporale Cosmo Fragnito, 205 Battaglione Chimico Mortaio, recounts:

The day after the armistice, at about five in the morning, the barracks in which my *battaglione* was billeted were surrounded by German and Fascist soldiers who ordered us to lay down our arms. We refused to comply, and soon gunfire erupted and in the ensuing mêlée I was wounded twice on one of my legs and once slightly in the left genital member. My *battaglione* eventually surrendered about 11.30 a.m. and since there were casualties on both sides the Germans allowed medical attendants to pick up the wounded and transport them for treatment. I was taken to Celio Hospital in Rome. Many of the friends in my unit who had also taken part in this fighting but who had not been wounded were not so lucky – they were sent to Germany as prisoners.

Many other soldiers shed their uniforms and melted into the civilian population, while others escaped and joined partisan groups in the mountains. Tenente

Italian soldiers are disarmed by Germans of the 2nd paratroop division during an operation codenamed Achse, after the 8 September 1943 armistice. (Bundesarchiv, Koblenz)

Claudio Andreanelli remembers:

In September 1943 I was an instructor for new recruits in Macerata in central Italy. My superior officer ordered me to surrender to the Germans and give them my Beretta pistol. I was locked in a room with other officers but escaped and headed into the mountains. I joined a local partisan group, where I adopted the battle name of Sergio. My wife and two children had to exist for nearly a year without money, not knowing what had happened to me. I was not united with her again until the Allies liberated Macerata in 1944.

The vast majority of Italian soldiers were captured and some 615,000 were shipped to internment camps in Germany. There they faced either slave labour or enlistment in combat units of the new German-backed Fascist regime in northern Italy. Only about 1 per cent joined their former allies. Of those who remained in the camps, 30,000 eventually died of hunger, exposure or overwork.

Alpino Tullio Lisignoli recounts:

On the night of 8 September 1943, a German officer came to our camp, which was near Fortezza in the Brennero Pass area, northern Italy. He went to the tent of our commander, Tenente Garaboldi, and spoke to Tenente Trentanni, another officer who was also present and who spoke very

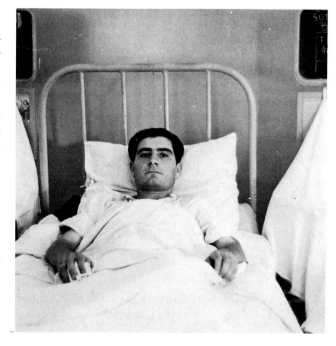

Corporal Cosmo Fragnito in Celio hospital, Rome, recovering from wounds inflicted during a battle with German and Fascist soldiers the day after the 8 September 1943 armistice was announced. (Author's collection)

good German. The German said, 'It's over [Italy had just capitulated]. You must drop all your arms.' Tenente Trentanni replied 'No! Never.' The German pulled out his pistol and shot him. After this Tenente Garaboldi went out and ordered everyone to drop their weapons and go to the train waiting to take us all home. We were loaded into the wagons. The doors were closed but the Germans then turned the train around and steamed towards Austria. We were now prisoners of the Germans . . . .

We were put into a POW camp, Stalag 17, where a German officer addressed us. He said, 'We know a lot of you Italians were in Russia fighting with the Germans, and we want you to join us again to fight the Russians. But we said,

'No, we are finished. We don't want any part of that. We don't want any more to do with the war.'

The next day, as prisoner 90794, I was sent with a group of 2,000 others to a factory in Linz, Austria, which made heavy tanks. I spent the rest of the war in various parts of Austria as a slave labourer before finally being liberated by the Americans in Salzburg in April 1945.

Blackshirt Antonio D'Angelo relates:

I returned to my home town of Pratola Peligna in the province of L'Aquila [central Italy] during September 1943 after service in the Border Militia. The town was occupied by the Germans. I served for a short time in a local pro-

Colonel Giuseppi Priscobio with men of the 208 infantry depot cross over to the allied lines after a 90-kilometre trek through the mountains of Calabria. 25 September 1943. (Author's collection)

Fascist unit called Brigata Maiella. Named after the highest mountain in the region, the unit was made up of ex-Arditi and MVSN. By this time I had two children and my wife was pregnant with a third, so that was the end of my military career. I took part in several black market and clandestine operations to survive and feed my family until the end of the war in May 1945.

Cosmo Gaetano of 5 Reggimento d'Armata Artiglieria:

I was stationed at Sassolungo in Albania and on 9 September the Germans captured our commander, General Dalmazio, forcing him to sign a surrender document.

The Germans disarmed our artillery weapons by taking the breech-blocks off. Then they ordered us to walk miles to the nearest railway station, where we were loaded on to open wagons and taken to Germany, a journey that took ten days.

I was first sent to the Dortmund POW camp [near the town of the same name] and from there to the concentration camp of Elsental near Essen. Inside the camp was an iron factory in which I worked until it was liberated by the Americans on 8 April 1945.

Capitano Enrico Buffoni:

In March 1943 I was wounded near Wadi Akarit on the Tunisian front and captured by elements of the 8th Army. I spent a few weeks in Alexandria, then was sent to POW Camp 316 in Geneifa, Egypt.

In late 1943, the Italian army obtained an armistice, and soon after joined the Allies in actual combat against the Germans. It was real fighting, and we took a very heavy toll of losses. The war cemetery of Monte Cassino has many thousands of Italian and Polish names on its crosses.

During 1943 the King of Italy issued an invitation to all Italian POWs to join the war effort alongside the Anglo-Americans. It was a strictly personal choice, not an order. So many thousands of Italian POWs in camps in Kenya, Egypt and India became 'co-operators'.

These units were made up entirely of Italian personnel, with the official ranks they held in the Italian army. The majority of these Italian co-op units were used in Egypt and Kenya. They worked in the REME shops, in the NAAFI transport, in harbour and aircraft maintenance, some in the British navy.

I was with the 2618 Italian Co-op Unit, Benghazi Naval Base, for a few months. Then I was called to Cairo HQ as 'Liaison', which in army lingo means just interpreter.

As you can imagine, I had a wonderful time in Cairo. But I want to stress the point that these co-operators' units performed excellent work, with high spirits and strict discipline. Many times I received compliments from British HQ officers for the unexpected efficiency of our units. The answer was that 'now we feel we are on the right side of the ditch'.

Aldo Bacoccoli 7 Reggimento Bersaglieri, Divisione Motorizzata Trento, reflects:

I was captured on 10 July 1942 by New Zealand soldiers who attacked our sector near El Alamein, Egypt. I had been wounded and so was transferred to a New Zealand field hospital where a bullet was extracted from my neck. I was then taken to a hospital in Alexandria.

I was surprised to find in the hospital what looked like an Indian Sikh holy man, who helped endlessly all the wounded soldiers. Later a young and pretty nurse came into my ward by the name of Dauletta. Perhaps due to the fact that I had a steel front tooth which she noticed, I was the centre of little attentions by the pretty nurse. Attentions which I will add upset my balance and caused my blood to boil like a volcano.

One day she gave me a pot full of thermometers and brushed her body slightly against me, which was enough to drive me crazy. I dropped the thermometers and was subsequently accused of sabotage and ended up being transferred to a POW camp in South Africa.

The camp was Zonderwater, known as 'the kingdom of the fleas', in which I was to spend two years. I remember an old guard was inspecting a very deep latrine ditch which had been dug by us POWs; he suddenly found himself alone and without a ladder at the bottom of the ditch and was not allowed to climb out unless he shouted 'Viva il Duce!'

The South African army captain in charge of X block in which I was confined used to ride a beautiful horse until one day some POWs shaved the poor horse leaving only a few hairs which were showing the words 'Viva il Duce!'

After two years in South Africa I spent the rest of the war in POW camps in England, Wales and Scotland before returning home to my family in Perugia.

The citizens of Scafati near Naples burn Fascist books and emblems in the town square, 1 October 1943, after being liberated by the Anglo/US Fifth army. (Author's collection)

Glossary

A NOI – slogan, 'With Us'

AB (Autobilinda) – Armoured car

ACHSE – (Axis) – German codename for the disarming of Italian military forces after the 8 September 1943 armistice

AGF – (Avanguardisti Giovani Fascisti) – Fascist Youth Vanguards. One of the first Fascist youth organisations

Al Valore Militare – Military Valour

Alpini – Elite Alpine soldiers of the Royal Army

Alpino – Singular of Alpini

AM – Military Administration

Arditi – Originally World War I Italian shock troops

Ariete – Battering ram (also name of Armoured Division in North Africa)

Artiglieria – Artillery

Artiglieria d'Armata – Heavy artillery

Artiglieria Divisionale – Divisional Artillery

Artiglieria Marittima – Marine artillery

Autobilinda – Armoured car

Avanti – Forward! – The socialist newspaper of which Mussolini was editor until his expulsion from the socialist party

Baistrocchi – a style of grey-green tunic with an open collar named after General Baistrocchi, Secretary of War

Balilla – Fascist Youth organisation for eight- to eleven-year-olds

Battaglione – Battalion

Battaglione Fanti dell'Aria – Infantry of the Air Battalion

Battaglione Nazionale Paracadutisti – National Parachute Battalion

Bersagliere – Singular of Bersaglieri

Bersaglieri – Elite corp of sharpshooters

Breda – Italian arms manufacturing company

Brigadieri – Sergeant

Brigata – Brigade

BTG. CCNN – Blackshirt battalion

Bustina – envelope, reference to the style of side cap worn by Italian army

Capitano – Captain

Carabinieri Reali – Military police, senior arm of the Royal Army

CCNN – Plural of CN (Camice Nere), Black Shirt

CCRR – Plural of CR (Carabinieri Reali)

Celere – Fast, quick

Centauro – Centaur, mythical creature with man's head, trunk, and arms, and a horse's body and legs

Centesimi – Unit of Italian currency

Chimico – Chemical

Chimico Mortaio – Chemical mortar

Cohort – Equivalent to a battalion

Comando Generale – General Headquarters

Compagnia – company

Com. Milizie. Controaeri Artg. Marittima – Headquarters of the anti-aircraft and maritime artillery

Console Generale – Militia equivalent of a brigade general of the Royal Army

Controaeri – Plural of *Controaera*, anti-aircraft

Corazzato – Armoured

Corazzieri – Cuirassier, cavalry who wear armoured breastplates

Cordellino – Fine braided material used in the manufacture of officers' tunics and breeches

Corso Allievi Ufficiali – Officer Cadet Course

Croce al Valore Militare – Military Valour Cross

DAK – Deutsches Afrika Korps, two German divisions sent to North Africa early 1941 under command of General Rommel

Divisione – Division

Duce – Leader, title often used for Benito Mussolini

Falangist – Anti-communist Spanish forces commanded by General Francisco Franco

Fanteria – Infantry

Fasci all' Estero – Overseas Fascists

Fascio – Symbol of the Fascist Party, a bundle of rods tied together with an axe

FGC – (Fasci Giovanili di Combattimento) – Groups of Young Combatants. Fascist youth group for eighteen- to twenty-one-year olds

Fiat Spa – Motor vehicle manufacturer based in Turin, northern Italy

Folgore – Lightning bolt

GAF – Guardia alla Frontiera – Frontier Guard

GAL – (Gioventu Araba del Littorio) – Arab Fascist Youth

Generali – Officers of general rank

Generale – Singular of Generali

Generalfeldmarshall – Field Marshal

Gil (Gioventu Italiana del Giovani Fascisti) – Young Fascists

Giovani Fascisti – Young Fascists

GNR (Guardia Nazionale Repubblicana) – National Republican Guard

Granatieri – Grenadiers

Greca – Zigzag braid on Royal Army general's peak cap

Greca Littoria – Zigzag braid worn on peaked cap by Fascist Militia generals

Gruppo – Group

Guardia di Finanza – Finance Guard

Guardia alla Frontiera – Frontier Guard

Guastatori – Assault Engineers

Guida – Guide

Heer – Army (German)

Kriegsmarine – Navy (German)

Legione – Legion, equivalent to a regiment

Libica – Libya

Lira – Unit of Italian currency

Littorio – Fascist rod and axe

Luftwaffe – Air force (German)

Lugotente Generale – Militia equivalent of an army corps general of the Royal Army

L6/40, L3/33, M11/39, M13/40 – The Italian designation for armoured vehicles was L for light and M for medium, the first numeral the weight in tons and the last two numerals the year of introduction e.g. L3/33 was a light tank of three tons introduced in 1933

MAB – Moschetto Automatico Beretta – Beretta Automatic machine-gun

Manganello – short, stout wooden cudgel used by Fascist *squadristi*

Maresciallo – Field Marshall or senior warrant officer

Merito di Guerra – War merit

Milizia Confinaria – Frontier Militia

Milizia di Frontiera – Frontier Militia

Milizia Forestale – Forestry Militia

Milizia Controaerei – Anti-aircraft militia

Milizia Universitaria – University Militia

Milizia Postelegrafonica – Post and Telegraph Militia

Milizia Portuaria – Port Militia

Milizia Naz. della Strada – National Road Militia

Mortaio – Mortar

Motomitraglieri – Motorised machine-gunners, on motorcycles

Motorizzata – Motorised

MT – Motor Transport

MVSN (Milizia Volontaria per la Sicurezza Nazionale) – Volunteer Militia for National Security

NAAFI – Navy, Army and Airforce Institutes. Canteens ran by this organisation for servicemen.

Nappine – Tuft, pom-pom worn on Alpine-style cap

Nebbiogeni – Fog or mist

Nembo – Cloud burst, shower of rain

ONB (Opera Nazionale Balilla) – Balilla National Organisation, Part of the Fascist Youth

OND (Opera Nazionale Dopolavoro) – Fascist institution organising the after-work leisure activities of Italians

OTO (Odero Terni Olando) – one of the companies that manufactured anti-personnel hand grenades

Plotone – Platoon

Popolo d'Italia (The Italian Nation) – Newspaper started by Mussolini in 1914 in opposition to the socialist publications

Portuaria – Port (adjective)

Presente – present

Rancio – military rations

Raggruppamento/Raggruppamenti – grouping, somewhat like a modern task force used by the US armed forces

Reali – royal

Reggimento – Regiment

Reggimento Fanti dell'Aria – Infantry Regiment of the Air

Regio Esercito – Royal Army

RSI (Repubblica Sociale Italiano) – Italian Social Republic

Sahariana – Style of tropical tunic popular in the African colonies and Italy

Savoia – Name of the Italian royal family

Sergente Maggiore – Sergeant-Major

SRCM (Societa Romana Costruzioni Meccaniche) – Name of one of the companies that manufactured anti-personnel hand grenades

Sotto Tenente – Second Lieutenant

Sottufficiale – Singular of Sottufficiali
Sottufficiali – Italian non-commissioned officers
Squadristi – Bands of Fascist Blackshirts
Tenente – Lieutenant
Tenente Colonello – Lieutenant-Colonel
Truppa/Truppe – other ranks
TS (Truppe Speciale) – Troop special
Ufficiale – Italian officer
Ufficiali – Italian officer corps
Universitaria – University (adjective)
Valore Militare – Military Valour
Viva il Duce – Long live the leader
Wehrmacht – Armed forces (German)
Zona – Zone, the recruiting area of a MVSN division

3 Gennaio – 3 January 1925. Date when Mussolini assumed full powers in parliament by muzzling the opposition parties (though not yet officially banning them), in effect becoming dictator from that date.
1 Febbraio – 1 February 1923, the date when the MVSN was officially formed
23 Marzo – 23 March 1919. The date of first meeting when Fascist party was founded
21 Aprile – 21 April. Date decreed as a Fascist holiday
28 Ottobre – The anniversary of the march on Rome, 28 October 1922, which sparked the rise of Fascism as a national power

Bibliography

Adams, Henry, *Italy at War*, USA and Canada, Time-Life Books Inc., 1982

Belogi, Ruggero, *Regio Esercito Italiano Uniformi 1933–1940*, Italy, 1978

Benussi, Giulio, *Armi Portatili Artiglierie e Semoventi del Regio Esercito Italiano 1900–1943*, Milan, Intergest, 1975

Brook-Shepherd, Gordon, *Royal Sunset: The Dynasties of Europe and the Great War*, London, Weidenfeld & Nicolson, 1987

Campbell, Christy, *The World War II Fact Book 1939–1945*, London and Sydney, Futura Publications, 1986

Chamberlain, Peter and Gander, Kerry, *Axis Pistols, Rifles and Grenades – WWII Fact Files*, London, MacDonald & Janes, 1976

Cioci, Antonio, *Il Reggimento 'Giovani Fascisti' Nella Campagna dell'Africa Settentrionale 1941–1943*, Bologna, 1980

Clifford, Alexander, *Three Against Rommel*, London, George C. Harrap, 1944

Collier, Richard, *Duce! The Rise and Fall of Mussolini*, London, Fontana Books, 1972

Crociani, Piero and Viotti, Andrea, *Le Uniformi Coloniali Libiche 1912–1942*, Italy, La Roccia, 1980

Cumpston, J. S., *The Rats Remain: The Siege of Tobruk, 1941*, Melbourne, Grayflower Productions, 1966

Del Boca, A., *La Guerra d'Abissinia (1935–41)*, Italy, Feltrinelli, 1965

Del Boca, A., *Gli Italiani in Africa Orientale*, Italy, Laterza, 1979

Del Giudice, Elio and Vittorio, *Italiani . . . Tutti in Divisia!*, Parma, Tuttostoria, 1980

Del Giudice, Elio and Vittorio, *Atlante Delle Uniformi Militari Italiane dal 1934 ad Oggi*, Bologna, Albertelli, 1984

Fisch, Robert, *Field Equipment of the Infantry 1914–1945*, USA, Greenberg Publishing Company, 1989

Goglia, Luigi, *Storia Fotografica dell'Impero Fascista*, Italy, Laterza, 1985

Hibbert, Christopher, *Benito Mussolini*, London, Reprint Society Ltd, 1963

Hogg, Ian and Weeks, John, *Military Small Arms of the Twentieth Century*, London, Arms & Armour Press, 1973

Holt, Bob, *From Ingleburn to Aitape*, Lakemba, NSW, R. Holt, 1981

Lundari, Giuseppe, *I Paracadutisti Italiani 1937/45*, Italy, Editrice Militare Italiana, 1989

Marzetti, Paolo, *Uniformi e Distintivi del'Esercito Italiano 1933–1945*, Parma, Albertelli, 1981

McGuirk, Dal, *Rommel's Army in Africa*, London, Stanley Paul, 1987

Mirouze, Laurent, *World War II Infantry in Colour Photographs*, London, Windrow and Green, 1990

Pericoli, Ugo, *Le Divise del Duce*, Milan, Rizzoli, 1983

Piekalkiewicz, Janusz, *The Cavalry of World War II*, New York, Stein & Day Publishers, 1980

Pignato, Nicola, *Artiglierie e Automezzi dell'Esercito Italiano nella Seconda Guerra Mondiale*, Parma, Albertelli, 1972

Pignato, Nicola, *Le Armi Della Fanteria Italiana nella Seconda Guerra Mondiale*, Parma, Tuttostoria, 1978

Riccio, Ralph, *Italian Tanks and Fighting Vehicles of World War II*, England, Pique Publications, 1977

Rosignoli, G., *MVSN 1923–1943*, Surrey, Rosignoli, 1980

Rosignoli, G., *Ribbons of Orders, Decorations and Medals*, Poole, Dorset, Blandford Press

Rosignoli, G., *Alpini*, Parma, Albertelli, 1989

Salvatici, Luciano, *Pistole Militari Italiane (Regno di Sardegna e Regno D'Italia 1814–1940)*, Florence, Editoriale Olimpia, 1985

Scandaluzzi, Franco, *Inquadramento della MVSN e sue Unita Combattenti 1923–1943*, Italy, privately published 1985

Scandaluzzi, Franco, *Story and Insignia of the Paratroops in the Italian Armed Forces 1938–1970*, privately published

Smith, Denis Mack, *Mussolini*, London, Weidenfeld & Nicholson, 1981

Smith, W. H. B., *Small Arms of the World*, London, Arms & Armour Press, 1973

Stephens, Frederick J., *Italian Fascist Daggers*, London, Militaria Publications, 1972

Stephens, Frederick J., *The Collector's Pictorial Book of Bayonets*, London, Arms & Armour Press, 1976

Tunney, Christopher, *Biographical Dictionary of World War II*, London, J. M. Dent & Sons Ltd, 1972

Viotti, Andrea, *Uniformi e Distintivi dell'Esercito Italiano nella Seconda Guerra Mondiale 1940–1945*, Rome, Stato Maggiore dell'Esercito Ufficio Storico, 1988

War History Branch, Department of Internal Affairs, *Takorouna*, Wellington, 1951

Watts, John and White, Peter, *The Bayonet Book,* Birmingham, 1975

Weeks, John, *World War II Small Arms,* London, Orbis Publishing, 1979

Wiskermann, Elizabeth, *The Rome-Berlin Axis,* London and Glasgow, The Fontana Library, 1966

Windrow, Martin, *World War Two Combat Uniforms and Insignia,* Cambridge, Patrick Stephens Ltd, 1977

Periodicals

Amici Nel Mondo, Vol 2, Issue 3, March 1990. 'The Last Cavalry Charge in World War II' by Sergio Andreanelli

Uniformi & Armi magazine. No. 6 October 1989

Campaigns magazine No. 27 Vol 5, March/April 1980, 'The Italian Army in Africa'

I Bersaglieri, Rivista Militare – Quaderno 4

Various issues of NZ Returned Services Association Journal, *The RSA Review*

The Military Advisor, Winter, 1989. 'The Presentation Dagger of the Fascist Militia – MVSN

Pre-War and Wartime Publications

Badoglio, Pietro, *La Guerra d'Ethiopia,* Milan, A. Mondadori, 1936

Ministero Dell'Interno, *Milizia Volontaria per la Sicurezza Nazionale, Istruzione per la Divisia degli Ufficiali e Truppa e Regolamento sulla Uniforme,* Milan, 1923

Regolamento sull'Uniforme e Istruzione sulla Divisia del RR.Corpi di Truppe Coloniali, Rome, Ministero Delle Colonie, 1929

Regolamento sull'Uniforme e Istruzione sulla Divisa della MVSN, Rome, 1931

Milizia Volontaria per la Sicurezza Nazionale Comando Generale, Istruzione sull'Uniforme della MVSN (Ufficiali, Sottufficiali e Camicie Nere), Rome, 1941

Uniformi e Distintivi degli Ufficiale Sottufficiali delle Truppe D'Africa, Libiche e Coloniali, Ministero Dell'Africa Italiana Ufficio Militare, 1938–1940

PNF Gioventu Italiana del Littorio Comando Generale, Regolumento sulle Uniformi, 1942

Addestramento della Fanteria Vol 1, Ministero Della Guerra, Rome, 1936

Ministero Della Guerra, *Raccolta di Disposizioni Permanenti, in Vigore per il R. Esercito,* Rome, 1910

Sales Catalogue of F. M. Lorioli Fratelli, Milan, 1938

Africa Orientale Italiana, Consociazione Turistica Italiana, Milan, 1938

Handbook on the Italian Military Forces, Military Intelligence Service, Washington DC, 3 August 1943

Handbook on the Italian Army (Provisional Copy), US Army Map Service, 22 May 1943, reprinted by Athena Books, Great Britain, 1983

Notes on Enemy Army Identifications – Italy, British Military Intelligence, October 1941

Arthur F. Loveday, *World War in Spain,* London, John Murray, 1939

Eric Rosenthal, *The Fall of Italian East Africa,* 1941

The Abyssinia Campaigns, His Majesty's Stationery Office, London, 1942

Conrad Norton and Uys Krige, *Vanguard of Victory – A Short Review of the South African Victories in East Africa 1940–1941,* Union of South Africa Government Printer, Pretoria, 1941

The Eighth Army, His Majesty's Stationery Office, London, 1944

Soldier's Guide to Italy, 1944

Middle East Training Pamphlet No. 10 'Lessons of Cyrenaica Campaign' 409/GHQP/8,500/4–42

Italy, Education Rehabilitation Service 2 NZEF

J. F. Horrabin, *1939 News Maps,* Victor Gollancz Ltd, London, 1939

Unpublished Italian Military memoranda of the Italian Army 1922–1943 in the author's possession and kindly loaned

Official Collections

Archives of the 21 NZ Infantry Battalion Association held in the Association's Clubrooms, Fearon Park, Auckland, New Zealand

Military photographic archives of the Bundesachiv, Koblenz, Germany

Military photographic archives of the Alexander Turnball Library, Wellington, New Zealand

Original and microfilm copies of documents in the New Zealand National Archives relating to the Italian military forces in North Africa 1940–1943 (War History Collection, Wellington, New Zealand)

Index

Aden Pattern 105
Administration Service 54
Alpine Caps 106-107
Alpini 40, 64, 65, 98, 106, 107, 138, 144
Andreanelli, Tenente Claudio 30, 37, 154
Anti-Aircraft Coast Defence Militia 54, 148
Aosta, Duke of 52
Armoured Divisions 43
   131 Centauro 45
   132 Ariete 45
   133 Littorio 45
Arm Shields 143-147
Artillery: Model 35 20/65 AA Gun 110
   Model 37 47/32 Anti-Tank Gun 110
   65/17 Infantry Gun 111
Artillery Service 109
Assault Engineer School 48
Automobile Service 55

Bacoccoli, Aldo 156
Badoglio, Maresciallo 50
Badoglio, Pietro 53
Baistrocchi, General Federico 60
Baistrocchi Pattern 60, 61
Balbo, Governor Italo 46
Bastico, Generale Ettore 27, 31
Bayonets and Combat Daggers 126-128
Beretta: Model 34 129
Bersaglieri 41, 45, 64, 65, 72, 98, 100, 105, 108, 138
Bersaglieri Regiment: No 9 22
   No. 10 11
   No. 11 11
Blackshirt Legion 40
Binoculars 133
Bir el Gobi 22
Bonechi, Sergente Maggiore Luigi 29
Breda, M30 130
Buffoni, Capitano Enrico 30, 156
Burials and Graves 35-38
Bustina 102-104, 108

CCRR: Carabinieri 23-24
CCNN 148
Camouflage 70
Carcano M1891 126, 129
Carlo Alberto, King 141
Cavallero, Generale 32

Cavalry charge 43
Celere Divisions 41
Central Carabinieri School 29, 32
Chemical Troops 49
Cigarettes 35
Cioci, Antonio 22, 28
Cocchi, Tenente Giorgio 22
Collar Patches and Devices 137
Colonial Militia 51, 52, 126
Combat Uniforms 59-72
Commissariat Service 54
Compasses 133
Conscription 18
   training 25-33
   leave 29
Continental Peaked Caps 100
Continental Side Caps 102
Continental Uniforms 60-66
Cordellino 60, 62, 63, 66, 68
Crash Helmets 100

Dalmazio, General 156
D'Angelo, Antonio 21, 22, 23, 25, 29, 37, 137, 155
De Giorgis, Generale 32
Doctrine 39-40

Elena, Queen 13
Engineers 8
Ethiopian Campaign 22-23
Evaluation book 135

FNA Breschia 124
Facist Albanian Militia 52
Facist Militia – see MVSN
Facist Movement 12, 14, 15-17, 18, 20
Facist Youth Organisations 16, 17, 126
Facta, Luigi, Prime Minister 12
Fassio, Sotto Tenente Guiseppe 22
Festa, Tenente Guiseppe 32, 33
Fez 108
Field Artillery 47
Field Dressing 132
Finance Guard 24
Footwear – Continental 64
   Tropical 69
Forestry Militia 53, 148
Fragnito, Caporale Cosmo 153

Franceschini, Generale 32
Franco, General 22
Frontier Guard 24, 50-51, 54, 144, 148

Gaetano, Cosmo 35, 156
Garaboldi, Generale Italo 33
Garaboldi, Tenente 33, 151, 155
Gas Masks 131
Giachi 22
Glisenti Revolver 128, 129
Gloves 66
Grandi, Dino 153
Graziani, Marshall 50, 137
Greatcoats, Continental 64

Hand grenades 112-113
Haversacks 130-131
Headwear 97-108
Highway Militia 54
Hitler, Adolf 153
Holsters and Bandoliers 128-130
Holt, Bob 'Hooker' 28

Ice Axe 132
Identity Discs 143
Individual Record Book 135
Infantry Divisions 40
Italian Expeditionary Corps 43

Kesselring, Albrecht 153
Knapsacks, Rucksacks and Haversacks 130-131

Liberal Party 12
Lisignoli, Alpino Tullio 25, 33, 37, 154
Lorioli & Castelli 144

MVSN Identification Booklet 136
MVSN: Milizia Volontaria Per la Sicurezza
    Nazionale 51, 60, 61, 63, 64, 65, 66, 67, 72, 98,
    102, 103, 105, 106, 107, 108, 126, 127, 129,
    147, 148
Machine-guns 118-123
    Model 301 (Breda) 118
    Model 37 (Breda) 118
    Model 14 (Fiat-Revelli) 121
    Model 35 (Fiat-Revelli) 121
    Model 38A Moschello Automatico 121
Mannlicher Carcano 124
Map Case 133
Medals 140-142
    Order of Precedence 142

Medical Service 55-57
Mess Tins 132
Military Chemical Service 49
Military Colleges: Ancona, Modena, Naples, Rome,
    Turin 30
Military Pay 137
Military Postal Service 137
Military Valour Medal 141-142
Militias 51
Militia Shields 147-151
Mobile (Cavalry) Divisions 41
Montezemolo, Tenente Colonello 32
Mortars: Model 35, 81 mm 112
    Model 35, 45 mm Briocia 112
Motorised Divisions 46
    Trento, Trieste 46
Mountain Infantry Division 40
Mussolini, Benito Amilcare Andrea 11, 13, 14, 51, 52,
    137, 153
Mussolini, Alessandro 11
Mussolini, Rosa 11

Nicolini, Mario and Ippolito 22

ONB 15, 16
OND 28
Officer Pay Book 136
Officer Training 30-33

Pantaloons and Breeches – Continental 61-62
    Tropical 68
Paratroops 46-47
Pay 136-137
Pith Helmets 104-106
Popolo d'Italia 12
Port Militia 53, 150
Post and Telegraph Militia 53, 150
Promotion for Officers 34
Protective Clothing 70

Railway Militia 52
Ranks 137
Rations 35
Reggimento Cavalleggeri d'Alessandria 43
Reggimento Fanti dell'Aria 69
Reggimento Giovanni Facisti 22, 33, 37
Reggimento Savoia Cavalleria 43
Regonini 22
RE Terni 124
Revolvers and Pistols 114-118
    Model 1889 Glisenti 114

Model 1910 Automatic 118
Model 34 (Beretta) 118
Rifles 124-126
Road Militia 148
Rommel, General Erwin 27, 32
Rucksacks 130-131
Ruffiuatti, Fedrico 135

Sabre 127
Sahariana 66, 69, 70
Savoia-Genova, Margherita 13
Scabbard 126
Shelter Quarters 132
Shirts – Continental 63
    Tropical 67-68
Small Arms and Field Equipment 109-133
Socialist Party 11
Spanish Civil War 22
Steel Helmets 97
Steiner, Colonel 48
Sweaters, Continental 63

Training 25-33
Transport Service 55

Trentanni, Tenente 154, 155
Tropical Peaked Caps 103
Tropical Side Caps 103
Tropical Uniforms 66-69
Trousers 68
Truck-Borne Infantry Divisions 40
Tunics – Continental 60
    Tropical 66

Umberto I di Savoia 13
University Militia 54, 148

Veterinary Service 57
Vittorio Emanuele III 13, 15, 52, 137, 153

Walking Stick 132
Warrant Officer and NCO Training 29
Warrant Officer and Officer Pay Book 136
Water Bottles and Mess Tins 132
Wilmot, Chester 28

Zone Shields – Fascist Militia 147